Charles Comfort Tiffany

The prayer book and the Christian life : or, The conception of the Christian life implied in the Book of common prayer

Charles Comfort Tiffany

The prayer book and the Christian life : or, The conception of the Christian life implied in the Book of common prayer

ISBN/EAN: 9783337263614

Printed in Europe, USA, Canada, Australia, Japan

Cover: Foto ©Lupo / pixelio.de

More available books at **www.hansebooks.com**

THE PRAYER BOOK
AND THE CHRISTIAN LIFE

THE PRAYER BOOK

AND

THE CHRISTIAN LIFE

OR THE

*Conception of the Christian Life implied
in the Book of Common Prayer*

BY

CHARLES C. TIFFANY, D.D.

ARCHDEACON OF NEW YORK

NEW YORK
CHARLES SCRIBNER'S SONS
1898

University Press:
JOHN WILSON AND SON, CAMBRIDGE, U.S.A.

PREFACE

THE contents of this little volume constituted the substance of the Bohlen Lectures delivered in Philadelphia in February, 1898. The matter has been somewhat differently arranged, the lectures having been subdivided and slightly enlarged in order to render the treatment of the theme more succinct and complete. The object of the treatise is to indicate the conception of the Christian Life which the Book of Common Prayer presupposes, elucidates, and strives to nurture. From the method of its nurture the character of the life is deduced. It was of course impossible, in treating of the services of the Prayer Book, not to make an interpretation of them, and in that interpretation all may not agree. The intention of the interpretation, however, is not polemical. It is simply to elucidate the characteristic features of life as religious by an exposition of the discipline to which the Prayer Book subjects it. It is hoped that the largeness, healthfulness, and genuineness of the Christian Life may, in some measure, be made clear by the practical comment of the Prayer Book upon it, and that the Prayer Book itself may be better appreciated and more diligently used as the fulness of its scope and the sanity of its method become apparent through the perception of its bearing upon life.

C. C. T.

October, 1898.

CONTENTS

Chapter		Page
I.	Unity in Variety of Religious Life	3
II.	Prayer the Root of the Christian Life	12
III.	Common Prayer indicative of Social Christian Life	25
IV.	The Christian Life as Intelligent	39
V.	The Christian Life as Rational	47
VI.	The Christian Life as Salvation	61
VII.	The Christian Life as influenced by the Holy Scriptures	72
VIII.	The Bearing of the Collects on the Christian Life	89
IX.	The Influence of the Christian Year on the Christian Life	97
X.	The Christian Life as Taught by the Sacrament of Baptism	113
XI.	The Lesson of Confirmation for the Christian Life	125

Chapter		Page
XII.	The Lord's Supper in its Bearing on the Christian Life	139
XIII.	Clergy and Laity—The Ministry of Instruction	153
XIV.	The Ministry of Consolation	163

THE PRAYER BOOK

AND THE CHRISTIAN LIFE

THE PRAYER BOOK

AND

THE CHRISTIAN LIFE

CHAPTER I

UNITY IN VARIETY OF RELIGIOUS LIFE

THE Book of Common Prayer has usually been treated with reference to its bearing on ecclesiastical, theological, and liturgical matters. It has been regarded chiefly as a thesaurus of devotional expression, of doctrinal definition, or of ecclesiastical tradition. As such it has been used as an armory from which church combatants have drawn the potent weapons for their conflicts in the various departments of polemical encounter. Its sources have been diligently traced, and its expressions have been minutely searched, to supply material for such controversial discussion, or for the disciplinary action attending it. Like the Lord's Supper, which was instituted to be a bond of union and has been made a chief storm-centre of contention and excommunication, the Prayer Book, fashioned to be a manual of worship inclusive, in its charity, of wide differences of apprehension, has often been turned into a barrier to part Prelate from Puritan, to divide High Churchmen from Low Churchmen, to dissever Christian people into parties rancorous and belligerent.

As, however, the Eucharist, apart from theories concerning it, forms in its positive content a point of contact and unity for all sorts and conditions of Christians, so the Book of Common Prayer, in its positive content, apart from theories supposed to lurk beneath its expressions, furnishes a ground of common sympathy and a bond of practical union among all sorts and conditions of Churchmen. The intention of this volume is wholly irenical. But one would be very inexperienced or very blind to suppose that this irenical purpose could be compassed by any attempt to reduce all religious life, or the true expression of it, to the dead level of one exact pattern, or by any effort to explain away those real differences of conviction which have always characterized the Christian Church. These distinctive apprehensions of piety are founded in diversity of moral temperament and mental constitution. From their persistence they promise to be permanent and must be reckoned with. The æsthetic or practical trend of the nature, the mystical or rational temperament of the individual, the subjective or objective bent of the mind, — these have always existed, and will presumably always manifest themselves as existent in that department of life we call religious, as well as in that which we call secular. For these two departments of life, the religious and the secular, are to a Christian consciousness only subordinately two, being in reality but different sides of the one life in God. Men and women equally devout but unequally or diversely endowed have illustrated this natural and healthful divergence of type, while religion has persisted in them all. Any guide or directory of worship therefore which aimed at their suppression or extinction would prove abortive, and find itself discredited in its attempt to discredit a diviner order than its narrowness could descry. The attempt therefore will be to show that the Prayer Book offers a point of higher unity for the religious consciousness in its exposition of and contribution to the potent reality of the Christian life in all its varied forms.

There is nothing more apparent or impressive than the appearance and permanence of distinct types of Christian life; and it is well to recall the fact that they emphasize unity rather than disparity. The essential reality of religion is found to be in all of them and is in its signal vitality the germinal impulse of all typical divergence. Religious vitality is in fact too pervasive and intense in human nature not to manifest itself through any and every medium which may be present to it. It forces itself into prominence in manifold forms because no phase of individual endowment is strange or alien to its embrace. Just because it is so fundamental in human nature religion uses every channel which human nature offers through which to express itself, and cannot be restrained of expression any more than a sunbeam can be repressed in shining because the medium through which it shines happens to be blue or green or violet. The light of the sun is behind all the colors of the spectrum, and is manifest within them, and they all bear witness to the true light which lighteneth every color entering into the atmosphere which enwraps the world of vision. This analogy holds good in the realm of spiritual life, and the Book of Devotion, which would train the spiritual vision both to perceive and receive the divine light, must awaken and deepen the recognition of a common religious life in many divergent manifestations, and acknowledge an essential unity of religious hope and aspiration in manifold varieties of expression. Otherwise it could never be a Book of *Common* Prayer.

The permanence, however, of variety in types of religious character need not introduce permanent confusion into our idea of a common religious life, or of its value and eternal significance for every individual as for the whole race. The peaceable fruits of righteousness, ripened in varying atmospheres of religious devotion, vindicate their genuineness, though their special forms and flavors may suggest also their limitations and deficiencies. The mystic and the rational thinker; the man submerged in the flow of subjective emotion, and the man buttressed by the strong conviction of objective truth; one whose whole instinct is practical action, and another whose irresistible trend is to theoretical speculation; all these, and many other types have vindicated their right to be by the beauty of their personal piety and by the value of their contributions to Christian thought, in its discrimination as well as in its application of Christian truth. Through all these divergences there has run one common constant stream of divine reality. The variance discernible in the individuals composing the Apostolic College, afterwards incorporated and expressed in schools or classes of men; the calm practicalness of James, the speculative elevation of John, the emotive ardor of Peter, the sagacious activity of Andrew, the reclusive devotion of Nathaniel, the doubting faithfulness of Thomas, the spiritual rationality of Paul; all this variance at the source has been, as it must ever be, repeated in the stream, as that has gathered volume from the rills poured into it all along its course, until it has become the majestic movement of the River of God, which holds within its murmur the voice of many waters. How distinctively poorer the Christian world had been without the special gift and aptitude of Origen and Augustine, of Tauler and à Kempis, of More the Catholic and Leighton the Protestant, or in latter days in the Anglican Communion of Keble the sweet singer, and Arnold the strong teacher. Yes, within the compass of the Anglican Communion itself, without searching through the records of Oriental, or Roman, or German, or non-conforming English Christianity, the essential Christian life, in infinite and inspiring variety, has been fed and nurtured and strengthened by the manna from heaven gathered in this receptacle of the Book of Common Prayer. Every school has so really found there the food convenient for it that each variant type has claimed it for its very own. And the claim has been verified by the result, and is to be vindicated in all soberness because the Prayer Book has been to each type or school its own, while not merely its own. It has been so much to each because it has been more than each could discern, namely, the purveyor of that fundamental Christian life which underlies all types of Christian living and thinking, and is greater than them all, and which is so irrepressible and inevitable that it must press into and express itself out of all the variable conditions of the soul's existence. It is like nature, which carries its regnant law into the tropics as well as to the poles, indefinitely variable because indubitably one and insistent and indestructible. No circumstance is competent to circumscribe its activity, and no situation adequate to annihilate its vitality.

It is the contribution of the Book of Common Prayer to the development of this great underlying Christian life of all sorts and conditions of men which we are to consider in these pages. "And," to quote the admirable language of Bishop Gailor of Tennessee, "whatever else may be said of the type of Christianity which that book sets forth, it cannot be said that it is morbid or unhealthy or anything but sane in its views of man and God; or that its ideal is cramped and confined in the intellectual mould of any particular party or sect or set of men; or that the beauty of holiness and the standard of righteousness which it inculcates is less than sufficient for the high and noble and splendid satisfaction of human nature in its best endeavor for truth and freedom."

I judge that this will become apparent as we study the Book of Common Prayer more closely.

CHAPTER II

PRAYER THE ROOT OF THE CHRISTIAN LIFE

THE ideal of the Christian Life and the contribution of the Prayer Book to it is foreshadowed by certain features of that Book, which may be read in its title and seen before one opens its covers.

The Title is very significant. We have before us a Book of Common Prayer. Its effort to lead and educate the Christian flock is founded primarily in devotion, not in instruction. It is not chiefly a statement of the faith addressed to the understanding, though it contains a confession of the faith as an act of worship. Its appeal is to the heart and conscience through the act (which it essays to guide) of man's approach to God. If it be true that, as Neander held, "*Pectus est quod fecit Theologum*," the Prayer Book's unwritten motto is, "It is the heart which makes the Christian." Its very conception of the ideal of man's life is grounded on his right relation to God and right approach to him. Its system is Theo-centric. It finds the root of all true living not chiefly in man's external or natural relation to God, but essentially in his spiritual contact with Him. The physical law of man's natural environment is truly a Divine law, and is significant of a direct relation to God through man's physical life; and were this physical or natural relation regarded as chief it would involve, first of all things, the education of the natural faculties and an athletic discipline. But this, while important, is subsidiary. Nor is man's relation to God as Moral Governor the supreme relation even. This relation of moral accountability for our actions is intimate and sacred, and brings the soul into instant and conscious contact with God's mind and will, as expressed in the moral law. But the regulation of conduct yields in importance to the regulation of the heart and will from which conduct springs. That out of which proceed the issues of life indicates the point of ultimate contact of man with God. The supreme relation is the relation of the spirit of man to the Spirit of

God, the contact of person with person, the touch of the human individuality with the Divine Being. And all this finds the expression of its reality in the direct appeal of prayer and praise. It discovers the inspiration of its life in the apprehension of a Divine watch and ward, and the salutary control of life in the recognition of a Divine responsibility. In other words, according to the Prayer Book, Religion is the basis of the moral and ideal life of man; of which religion, Richard Whichcote wrote so finely in the seventeenth century, when he said, " Its seat is the inward man, it is the first sense of his soul, the temper of his mind, the pulse of his heart."

And this is quite in accord with the postulate of that rare philosophic thinker of the nineteenth century, Richard Rothe, who affirms in his Christian Ethics that the God-consciousness in man is the only explanation of his self-consciousness. For the self-consciousness of man only thoroughly comprehends itself when it realizes its dependence on the Divine, its correlation with the Divine, and its aspiration for the Divine. The underlying conception of the being whom prayer is to guide, elevate, and console is "Man as God's child." The ideal of his life is that eternal life which is to know God and Jesus Christ, whom He has sent. It is the life immortal held within the shrine of mortality. Duty to such a being can never be what some scientific inquirers into the genesis of morals catalogue it, "the sum of the prudential experiences of mankind." Its mandate is heard as the echo of that imperative voice of God which brings the eternal law of His own being into the sphere of man's temporal existence and so renders the earthly life eternal in its quality, a valid though transient manifestation of the eternal reality of God. The genesis of such a soul can never rest in its natural history. Like its Lord and Master, when once it has reached the final Adam it says of him "who was the Son of God." Its quality cannot be measured or gauged by the form or manner of its temporal development, by the stages which the physical organization of the race as of the individual may have passed through, by the refinement or the frailty of its mechanism, by the instruments it uses to plan, or think, or act, in fine, by the house in which it dwells. The master mind itself proclaims the sovereignty of the Spirit over the conditions which encompass it, and subordinates the limitations which these conditions impose on its action to the range of its own purpose, which it is restless to attempt even if it cannot wholly achieve its resistless impulse for advance and enlargement. Thus the very fact that a Book of Devotion is furnished as the essential nutriment of life proclaims the ideal of that life to be one which is God-given, God-controlled, God-crowned. It embodies by its very appearance the challenge of Tennyson's question, " What matters it how much a man knows and does if he keep not a reverential looking upwards? he is only the subtlest beast in the field then."

This vivid and practical apprehension of the Divine and the Eternal as the moulding germ of the ideal life of man gives tone to all the afterthought concerning man's culture and destiny. If it invests life with a solemnity of responsibility, it is yet the solemnity of high station and of boundless possibilities. It is not the solemnity of gloom and disheartenment such as comes and must come of an atheistic or agnostic conception of man, which finds no splendid purpose writ in his constitution, and no discernible or lasting outcome of his achievements or aspirations; which regards God simply as an unknown force which it is hopeless to resist, as it is hopeless to try in the least to comprehend; and which reduces humanity to a perpetual orphanage, since the lower creation cannot explain him, and the higher as constantly eludes him. If in his temporal existence man may even in a theistic conception be compared to the vapor or the flower, short-lived indeed, but whose origin we know and whose fruitfulness does not die with their disappearance, yet such a conception removes him far from the horror of being likened to a mere breath whose existence is simply a vibration of an all-pervading atmosphere, which vibration, as philosophers tell us, has existence but no being, its transitoriness being all there is of it as individually distinct from the general substance which underlies all things. The recognition of God in prayer is a recognition of relation, a relation which is not a servitude but a sonship; a relation of intercourse as well as of obedience. The recognition of prayer moreover is one of mutual relation. It recognizes not only that "in Him we live and move and have our being," absolutely and without limit, but also that relatively "in us He lives and moves and has His being." The two once recognized cannot exist apart, but must move on together. On man's part the voice of that mutual relation is prayer, —

> "A breath which fleets beyond this iron world,
> And touches him who made it."

On God's part it is Revelation by that eternal Word which lighteth every man coming into the world.

The ideal of our life then of which devotion is the ultimate factor is life not only given, controlled, and crowned by God, but also God-accompanied. It is an ideal which is fulfilled only by the worship which opens the heart and life fully and freely to the Divine influence and companionship. Prayer is the vital breath of this ennobled life, prayer which is, to quote the great Laureate once more, " like opening a sluice between the great ocean and our little channels, when the great sea gathers itself together and flows in at full tide."

All objections to the sanity of prayer are based upon an ideal of life below that which the Book of Common Prayer presupposes and holds up before us. If the human spirit is akin to the Divine, so as to recognize it and aspire toward it and find its own completion alone in it, then prayer as the expression of its longing is as natural and rational as a child's proffered supplication for his Father's love and guidance. It is pseudo piety by reason of its shallowness, though it take on the guise of reverence, to regard, as some natural philosophers would have us regard, prayer as an impertinent dictation of ignorance to supreme wisdom. The law of God by which he rules, say these, is fixed from the beginning in the reason of his own being, and therefore must be immutable and irresponsive to any and all appeal. But prayer is not the spirit's appeal against God's law which emanates from his being; it is the striving of the soul to come into full accord with that being, and so with the law which reveals him. Prayer simply discerns by its fine instinct that spiritual law which binds all spiritual life together and instinctively affirms life by spiritual intercourse and sympathy and companionship and request and response to be the imperative condition of its being, an uttermost law of life underrunning all special laws of its expression. The ultimate utterance of all prayer is, "My soul is athirst for God, for the living God: when shall I come and appear before God?" Thus in the Lord's Prayer, the pattern and condensation of all possible petition, which brings man's whole life of physical necessity, of moral need, of spiritual enlightenment and guidance, up into the realm of God's thought and benediction, the undertone of it all is that grand diapason, "Thy will be done." It is the voice vibrant with an irrepressible demand for spiritual unison with the central spirit which moves and lives in all things, never a petulant cry to subordinate God's decree of wisdom to man's impatience of His restrictive discipline.

Thus it is that the very possibility of prayer sets the ideal of life very high. It gives it an enduring spiritual reality which craves and cannot be content without that eternal life which is in the Father and in his Son, Jesus Christ. Hence life comes to light in its immortality in God, as its source is recognized as in him, and its sustenance as alone of him. It is revealed, to quote Whichcote once more, as "A Divine nature in us, a Divine assistance over us."

It was Lessing who said, with his characteristic sagacity, "Man's ideal never reaches beyond his Gods," and the ideal elevation of man which is the postulate of Prayer finds its reasonable basis in the nature and character of God which it implies. For He who heareth prayer is not a remote or an indifferent Deity. Impersonal force is not the occupant of the throne of the universe if that force have an ear to hear; nor does the intelligence which inhabits it sit apart in its impassiveness while only keen in its scrutiny. God who heareth prayer is not only "the King, eternal, immortal, invisible," though his being fulfils that majestic ascription of St. Paul. He is the father of the family of mankind. "He remembereth our frame, and considereth that we are dust"; and, "like as a father pitieth his children," stands ready to answer their appeal and draw them within the sphere of his loving communion. There is a kinship of mutual understanding involved in the offices of prayer, and there is involved an ascription of humanity to God, as well as of divineness to man in it. It makes humanity a reflection of the Divine in which God sees his image and is thus responsive to its appeal, and it gives a sacredness to all human attributes and relations to find their prototype in God. Out of this comes the possibility and the naturalness — so to speak in protest against the assertion of the impossibility and unnaturalness — of the Incarnation wherein God truly comes unto his own. Herein we find the ground of our Divine Master's claim not only of service but of heart companionship from his followers when he says, " I call you no more servants, but I have called you friends," — a relation we must deem impossible between Divine power and human weakness, were there not a nexus binding both in indissoluble union. Thus prayer, while it gives us the pervasiveness of pantheism, delivers us from its absorption of the Divine in the human, an absorption which would remove all play of free will homage from man's service to God, and involve God in all the moral aberration and sinfulness which the abuse of that free will creates in man; which would make God the repudiator of his own righteousness, unless sin is declared to be no sin.

So much we learn from prayer as petition. But praise is permanently involved in prayer as well as petition, because the undertone of prayer is praise, being the ascription of power to him whose aid is sought, and of the grace which will grant it, for without these two, might and love, prayer would be a plea to impotence or an appeal to an indifferent or a vindictive heart. He who proffers his request irresistibly exhales the incense of thanksgiving. The very attitude of prayer is adoration, and he who seeks by prayer to live in God's communion lives in that high realm of exultation which is exaltation; as the Apostle phrases it, a "sitting together in heavenly places," a "conversation which is in heaven," a "coming unto Mount Zion and an innumerable company of angels"; or as Bunyan quaintly describes it of his pilgrims, " a being in heaven before we get at it"; or, as Wordsworth translates it into the serene poetry of the Lake country, a "moving about in worlds not realized." That is, this praiseful element of life lends it a spiritual glow which witnesses to rays of light falling on it from beyond the sphere of sun and moon and stars,

> "Where every soul shines as the sun,
> And God himself gives light."

Thus the praiseful element of prayer imparts as it implies a conscious or unconscious enthusiasm, which makes life vital, and stimulates courage and endeavor. It brings also the peace of submission, because it has the witness in itself that life is not all of the earth earthy, imprisoned in physical forces, limited in its range to transient achievement, or as the fine old hymn has it, "vexed with trifling cares." And this because the soul can never find a full expression of itself in the mere reading aloud of its physical laws, but is impelled to utter its tribute of thanksgiving to Him whose outer garment the laws of matter weave, but whom himself to know alone satisfies its longing and is its eternal life.

CHAPTER III

COMMON PRAYER INDICATIVE OF SOCIAL CHRISTIAN LIFE

THE high ideal of life, which is involved in the thought of it as a life of which prayer and praise are the essential expression, is not and cannot be individual merely. It finds its full realization only in so far as it is communal, or involved with the life and movement of other men. So at least the title — for as yet we have not looked into its contents — of our Book of Devotion indicates. It is the Book of Common Prayer. It is the Book of the congregation, the Book not of the individual Christian only, but of the Church. It is, so to speak, not only the common property of Christians, but their property in common. They must, to fulfil its full purpose, use it together. As such it is distinguished from many of the manuals out of which it is made up. It implies the expectation of a common movement in worship, not merely of many separate acts of devotion in the same place, joined together in one only at some special crisis in the service to which each turns to give momentary attention and then lapses back to its own individual pre-occupation. This is the Roman use, from which the English service was reformed, when once the Anglican Communion threw off the bonds of the Papal authority. That practice has been eloquently defended and described by its advocates as the more life-like, the more comprehensive, the more natural. Such is Cardinal Newman's description of the service of the Mass, with its attendant congregation each absorbed in his own private devotion. "Each," he writes, "in his place, with his own heart, with his own wants, with his own thoughts, with his own intention, with his own prayers separate but concordant, watching what is going on, watching its progress, uniting in its consummation; not painfully and hopelessly following a hard form of prayer from beginning to end, but like a concert of musical instruments, each different, but concurring in a sweet harmony, we take our part with God's priest, supporting him, yet guided by him. There are little children there, and old men, and simple laborers, and students in seminaries, priests preparing for mass, priests making their thanksgiving, . . . but out of these many minds rises one eucharistic hymn, and the Great Action is the Measure and the Scope of it." The resonant bell sounds to call the attention to it. But the English service requires no bell to remind the congregation that a special part of the service is about to come. All are intent on the same office, all are moving together towards the one goal. The service at the altar is the people's service; the officiating priest is the mouthpiece of the attentive as well as attending priestly people. He is not doing something for them apart from them, most of which they cannot hear, none of which they need to follow. He is leading them. They hear and follow his voice, for it is not the voice of the stranger, it is theirs also. The introduction of the reminding bell in Anglican worship would be an inconsistent intrusion and a bald and senseless plagiarism.

For the English thought is to unite the people, to bring them through common worship to the recognition of their common life, the common life of devotion, and of ordinary association and intercourse. The pervasive unity of the Christian body is the basis of the Common Prayer. It is founded on the thought which St. Paul expresses, that "we are members one of another," so that if one rejoice or sorrow, all rejoice and sorrow with that one, and moulded on the idea Goethe so well expresses when he writes,

> "Es bildet ein Talent sich in der Stille
> Sich ein Charakter in dem Strom der Welt,"

which may be freely rendered,

> "A special gift may be evolved apart,
> But character amid life's common stream."

Common worship points directly to the ideal Christian life as led among one's fellow men; as a life of engagedness in life's common tasks, a life involved in the common yet divine relations of the family and of the state; a life in which diligence in business is not alien from fervency of spirit, but is a legitimate expression and illustration of "serving the Lord." The religious life is not by the Common Prayer marked off as the life especially of particular little communities, sets, sects, guilds, brotherhoods, conventual as bound by a restrictive rule; but rather as the broad life of humanity based on the moral rule of Christ's word and life, who himself came eating and drinking, was found in society as well as in the church, and sent his disciples into the world, not out of it. As he came into the world and sanctified marriage by his presence and first miracle, and into the workshop of Nazareth where he elevated the work of the hands into a daily living sacrifice of our powers to God, and mingled with the family life of the poor and the festivities and banquets of the rich, leaving the imprint of divine consecration on all of them, so the common worship of Him involves the common life in Him, and marks the lawyer, the physician, the merchant, the mechanic, the artist, the musician, as responsive to a divine calling, as well as the bishops, priests, and deacons, albeit in differing departments of the one great service of God. He who gives the cup of cold water is rendering as truly worshipful service to God as he who bears "the chalice of the grapes of God." He has met as distinct recognition in the words of the Master, and his reward is as distinctly spoken by his sacred lips.

As common worship indicates a common undertone of service in the Christian body whose members are variously occupied, so it suggests that view of worship in work which sanctifies the whole week and consecrates the outer temple of God's world, as well as the inner temple of the sanctuary which man has builded. And that view is this, that in every legitimate occupation, made legitimate by its ministry to the essential wants of man in the enlargement and enrichment of his capacity, which is God's endowment of his nature, we are to find an opportunity to meet God and receive his spirit into our life, according as our work is done in the spirit of Christ, as part of the soul's life in Him and in his world. In this view the common worship of the sanctuary indicates the common worship of life, so that man is never to view himself as apart from God, not merely because he is always living under his ken, but because he may be always rendering unto Him acceptable service and be always coming into direct unison with him. Of course this does not discourage or forbid certain offices and fraternities or sisterhoods, guilds, communities, as certain exigencies may arise requiring their special efficiency. But these are special for specific ends, and the Prayer Book knows them not. These come and go as the exigencies of life call out for them or call out against them. But the broad life of humanity goes on forever, the life of the family, the life of society, the life of business activity, the life of the state. These constitute the permanent religious sphere and those living in the pure discharge of their duties as a spiritual function are the Religious *par excellence*. Here we are to look for the great achievements in the Kingdom of Righteousness, which is the Kingdom of God, just as it is that along the hillsides and in the valleys and upon the broad plains, and not chiefly in the conservatories and glass houses, we are to look for the harvests which feed the world.

This common service as a common worship by humanity, suggested in the Common Prayer, indicates another correlated feature of the normal Christian life It is the service of God in the service of men, i. e. the going about doing good. To build the temple of a renewed soul is better than to build a cathedral; to regenerate a community or a corner of a community is to cause to be builded together as lively stones those in whom God dwells. The awful but benignant sanction of the judgment, as portrayed by Christ, is too emphatic to allow any one to blink at the worship of God contained in the kindly and helpful service of mankind. The Son of Man is discerned and served in the sons of men. And when the Divine Master picked out the imprisoned, the impoverished, the sick lying uselessly by in pain, as his especial representatives, he struck a note of hope for all men as he bade us go forth and minister unto them as unto him. We seem to see little of the Son of Man in these sons of men. But his eye pierced through all their degradation and criminality, through all their ignorant and stained condition, through all their pain and uselessness, and descried the secret shrine in every heart where the Divine

Word, which lighteth every man coming into the world, was whispering and striving to shine in the darkness which comprehended it not. Out of such he declares may come beings transformed by the renewing of their mind; so that they who walk in darkness may see a great light, and they who sit in the shadow of death unto them may the light shine. Thus the worship of ministry for him is not simply an expression of the lips, but an action of the life. It is hopeful and inspiring with its boundless possibility of bringing in "the Christ that is to be."

This common life of service in the world, foreshadowed by the life of common worship in the sanctuary, gives suggestive assurance also that the ideal of Christian life is life in a Kingdom of God here on earth. Safe transference to another sphere of being is not the Church's only end and aim. The great hereafter is indeed an object of anticipation and of preparation, but preparation for true life beyond is the preservation and propagation of true life here. This earth is the especial sphere of reality and duty now; and into it are to come the life and law of God, to transform it, not merely individual souls in it, but its manners, laws, principles, institutions, into an habitation of God through the spirit. Thus the kingdoms of this world shall become the Kingdom of God, a kingdom which while not of this world is to be in this world, the final answer to that fruitful prayer of word and work, "Thy Kingdom come." The ideal of the Christian life is the Kingdom of Righteousness, in the sense that society shall constitute a righteous organism founded in the truth, not in the mere expediency of transient policies. That Kingdom is not meant to be simply an instrument for the alleviation of temporal necessities, but a vehicle for permeating the whole life of the community and the state with the eternal principles of God's love and justice, so that he shall reign in it not merely by control as now, but as the inspiration of its life and the moulder of its manners, enshrined in its institutions, positively expressed in its laws, and alive and recognized in all the relations of its life, as these come to reflect the righteousness and mercy and purity and love which shone forth in the word and life of His well beloved Son. For the correlation of prayer is response, and the church is not forever to go on praying without an answer. The supplication, "Thy will be done on earth as it is in heaven," is not a phrase without a meaning, a wish deprived of certain expectation. In it the church passes out beyond itself, as a shrine of worship and spiritual discipline for individual souls, into the larger sphere of all man's interests and engagedness in the world, which it is to leaven with its own truth and grace until the whole be leavened. The normal Christian life is life in this Kingdom come and to come.

Thus we have lingered at the portal of the Book of Common Prayer, and read the inscription written on it, that we might gain some intimation of the Christian Life it presupposes and to which it seeks to minister. We shall open its covers and look at its pages in the next and following chapters to see how it fulfils the promise of its inspiring title.

CHAPTER IV

THE CHRISTIAN LIFE AS INTELLIGENT

ON opening the covers of the Book of Common Prayer, a glance at its pages reveals a suggestive element of its contents even before we read a single sentence of them. It is an English book, a circumstance which strikes us as inevitable in a manual written for the English race, but which, when the Prayer Book was compiled, was a startling innovation in the usage of Western Christendom. Latin is what any Churchman would have naturally been led to expect at that time, since in that language the services of the Church of Rome (which before the Reformation dominated Western Christendom) had for centuries been conducted. It may seem strange that the speech of a Pagan people should have become the ecclesiastical usage, and that, if a vernacular speech was not to be allowed in the worship of the Church, recourse was not had to the Hebrew or the Greek. The one was the language of the temple and the synagogue in which our Lord worshipped; the other the language in a dialect of which he spoke, and in which his Apostles wrote. Both these languages had become sacred to the Christian by their association with the revelation recorded in the Holy Scriptures. But the use of Latin points with unmistakable precision to the primitive practice of conducting worship even in Rome in a "language understanded by the people." The Church in Rome, which St. Paul in his Epistle addressed in Greek, became, as it grew, an integral portion of the Latin nation, which naturally used in its public devotions the language employed in secular life. Not even the nearness of the times of the Apostles nor the possession of Greek Gospels and Epistles brought with it an obligation to pray in a foreign or unknown tongue. For English speaking people to conduct divine service in the English language is thus a true following of the Apostles, is in fine the exact apostolic usage. Just as the true reproduction of an Englishman is not he who imitates him, for an Englishman imitates no one, but he who like him stands by his own traditions and is self-poised, so the true following of any example is always a following in the spirit. A slavish adherence to the letter often cramps or even kills the life which the letter once embodied and expressed. Ecclesiastical tradition however does not always follow the life giving principle of the Apostle, " Let all things be done unto edifying." Rome's ecclesiastical dominion grew, and it imposed its accustomed language on all over whom it came to rule. It was a sign of dominion on the one hand, and arguments of sentiment or utility supported it on the other. Latin was associated with the language of St. Peter, on whose chair the Pope assumed to sit, though of course St. Peter's familiarity with Latin is at least problematical, while his knowledge of Palestinian Greek is beyond question. And, besides sentiment, came in the argument of utility. It was urged as a bond of Catholic union that all Christian worshippers should worship in the same exact words. It was argued that the translation of sacred expressions and dogmas into many tongues might gradually change their sense and bring in heresies, an argument far more applicable to the preservation of creeds and dogmas in original manuscripts than to the prayers and praises of a popular assemblage of worshippers. And thus Latin maintained its monopoly of the language of the sanctuary, when it had ceased to be a living language, when none spoke it save scholars and statesmen, who added it as an accomplishment to the use of their native tongue.

The striking fact, then, that the Book of Common Prayer discarded the language of the existing missals and breviaries is very significant of its conception of the Christian life it would nurture and strengthen. That life was to be intelligent, and its devotion was not to root itself in superstition, but in knowledge. The use of English was a silent but strong assertion of the value of the worship of the mind. The Supreme Master had commanded men to love God with the mind, as well as with the heart and soul. That love, coming unto God in worship, must know that he is and what he is, "that he is the rewarder of such as diligently seek him." Man must worship God in truth as well as in spirit. He cannot acceptably use worship as an incantation or magic rite. His praying is not simply saying prayers. Worship is the expression of genuine desire, and to be acceptable must be the genuine language of the heart, not a mere formula. Our fathers, in accordance with this, said it must be understood. According to their conception, worship was not simply awe before an inscrutable power whom men should seek to placate by the flattery of importunate appeal. It was not the worship of an unknown God, to whom we address ourselves in an act of homage whose force and bearing we may not compute. The worship of God through Jesus Christ was to them a reasonable service. It is not, indeed, an act which plumes itself on the understanding of all mysteries, nor which pretends to fathom the depths of the Divine Being. It is not an assumption that all God's ways are known and plain to us, but it is founded on knowledge so far as that goes. It addresses itself to attributes in God's nature which it is assured do exist, and which the infinite content and range of the Divine nature beyond our knowledge do not contradict but immeasurably strengthen. The pattern of prayer set by the Master of all souls, while it comprehends all human wants, is marked by the directness and simplicity of a child. It asks, not wrestles, nor argues, nor cajoles, that it may receive. It does not batter down the door, but knocks at it. And it addresses the Divine from the basis of the human, in the quiet assumption of their coincidence. "Forgive as we forgive," it says, attributing the same disposition to the Heavenly as to the earthly Father, without presuming to limit His boundless mercy to man's imperfect and partial exercise of it.

In Christ, the Christian finds that the same quality which he shares with his fellow men is as really, while far more fully, resident in God; and it is on the basis of this known clemency of disposition that man rests his petition for forgiveness. As the prayer which the Lord Jesus set to be a pattern of devotion, as an example both of acceptable brevity and of the rational expression of known and recognized wants, as this simplest and grandest of forms is accompanied by a depreciation and denunciation of vain repetition and much speaking, it is quite evident that once praying it "with the spirit and the understanding also" is more pleasing to the Divine mind and more efficacious with the Divine will than the rattling discharge of a decade of Pater Nosters. In fine, the printing of the Prayer Book in the English tongue, to secure the intelligent and sincere devotion of the English worshipper, is in strict accord with the tone and temper of all that the New Testament has to say concerning the worship of God.

Thus in its conduct of common prayer the Prayer Book, like the Gospel, gives most significant suggestion of its ideal of the common Christian life. By its plea for intelligence, it seeks to bring the life out of the shadows of ignorance and credulity into the full sunlight of knowledge and conviction. It proclaims the marriage and forbids the divorce of faith, through which man appeals to God, and reason, through which God appeals to man. It incites to study and investigation because God's thought is thus disclosed to man's thought. It claims the earth whereon our life is led as the "Lord's with the fulness thereof," and regards even the physical instruments, as the telescope and microscope, which search into its wonders and reveal the Divine thought held in its bosom, as instruments fashioned for a sacred use, even the use of deciphering God's record of himself in the work of his hands. Such an intelligent faith is not afraid lest it peradventure be wrecked by the storms of controversy, for its Christ walks serenely on all these waters. The calm and assured faith in God, which underlies the very form of the Prayer Book's devotion as a reasonable service, renders futile all fear of banishing God from his universe by discovery or from his Bible by criticism. That terror is but a relic of the superstition which feared so much because it knew so little. The unexpressed but conscious postulate of the "Common Prayer writ in the native tongue" is that, as knowledge grows from more to more, more of that reverence, whose voice is worship, will dwell within the soul. The rational faith in which it is conceived fosters no dualistic scheme of nature without, or of the mind within. It lends no ear to the Manichean protest against matter, nor to the obscurantist protest against reason. It consequently feels no distrust of discoveries in the realm of nature, and would stimulate rather than discourage that wide survey and keen discrimination which in our day has created the world anew. The faith which the Prayer Book invokes and inculcates is one which could stand unshaken amid the earthquake shock of the Copernican system, that mightiest of natural revolutions. That scientific revolution in thought displaced our planet from the centre and transported it to the circumference of the solar system, and stigmatized as a speck of star dust what had been regarded as the central mass. It sent the earth spinning through space as the satellite of a system itself a satellite, though it had once seemed to be the immovable pivot of all celestial movement. So remote and insignificant a planet as the world was now declared to be, seemed to some to dwarf the importance of the race which dwelt upon it, and to render the assertion of God's dwelling among that race in the Incarnation of his Son an incredible audacity of religious arrogance. But faith allied to reason rested secure in the assurance that the infinite power which the new knowledge unfolded rendered it yet closer akin to the infinite love disclosed to faith in the Gospel. This divine visitation of the least of the stellar tribes seemed to comport yet more fully with the Master's word, about the search, by the head of the household, for the least lost coin of the treasury and the feeblest sheep of the fold. The steadfast faith in the unseen rested all the more secure in the conviction, that that revelation has not the least evidence for its verity which, though it humble man, exalts God.

Thus it is that the increasing knowledge of nature has its confirmation for the faith which penetrates beyond nature, and finds in it its ally, not its enemy.

Hence it comes that the normal religious life is one which is alert in intellect. If true to its Master it must recognize as his call that impulse within us which aims at the highest knowledge of nature and incites to the fullest discovery of the secrets locked in her bosom. It rejoices to believe that man touches the outer garment of the invisible spirit in the world of matter, from which touch there flows forth much healing of the mind. The careful scrutiny of Lyell among the rocks, the profound contemplation of the law of living things by Wallace and Darwin, the craving impulse of Nansen to penetrate the unknown within the icy regions of the pole, these to an intelligent faith are not irreligious longings, their curiosity is not impious, their pursuit is not demoralization. These enter in their research a high and noble realm where the Master accompanies, even as when he walked with the disciples through the Galilean fields and bade them consider the lilies how they grow, and mark the whirling flight of the birds in the sky, and know that the Father's thought and care were among them. Yes, Christ consecrates the intellect, and that consecration is not a lullaby, but an awakening. The stimulus to research and investigation, to discovery and contemplation, stirs in the voice which calls us to live on God's footstool as the Sons of God.

CHAPTER V

THE CHRISTIAN LIFE AS RATIONAL

AN intelligent Christian faith is intelligent in regard to the inner as well as the outer life of man. While it has no dread of nature or the science of it, it cherishes as well no obscurantist fear of the inner world of reason. It does not turn off from the realm of mind as from a region of false lights and delusive mirage, but rejoices to trust it as enkindled by the Divine Word "which lighteth every man coming into the world." To this inner conscience and consciousness it perceives, the Divine Word himself continually appealed. But while trusting this verifying faculty, as his Master trusted it, the wise householder, instructed unto the Kingdom of Heaven, recognizes the necessity to keep the inward eye clear lest the light in it become darkness. It does not therefore disregard the voice of the universal Christian reason, the conviction or the confession of the Church Catholic, or resist as irreconcilable with the voice within the claim of authority without which comes attesting the record of the ecumenical consciousness. But while it gives friendly reception to the utterance which claims the authority of the past, it tests it, that it may the better discover its meaning or detect its limitation, or mark how it holds in the germ that which now has come to fuller apprehension in the ripened experience of the race through the Divine leading.

For a reasonable faith holds that the Divine Word which has been ever speaking is speaking still, and that any ecumenical utterance finds its authority in the consenting conviction of the many voices which find expression in it. Thus to it the supreme witness to the truth is not simply truth as other men of other times have conceived it or uttered it, but that accord of the two voices of the past and of the present which discloses an undertone of concordant meaning in both, though the single note of the remoter time may have been modified in its emphasis or developed in its force as it is expressed in the fuller and more vibrant chord of to-day's utterance. To it legitimate theological thought does not assume the form of a mere archæological pursuit. It is not a study of fossils witnessing to an earlier life which has no vital connection with or development in the thought of to-day, and which we can only lament as extinct, and therefore strive to force ourselves back into it again. It rather holds Christian thought to be as legitimate to-day as yesterday, not as being cut off from yesterday, but as being an evolution out of previous life into nobler and more impressive or expressive forms.

And it learns this lesson from the progression of the race in faith and morals delineated in the Holy Scriptures, wherein the day spring from on high hath visited us as a shining light which shineth brighter and brighter unto the perfect day. This Scriptural witness to a gradual revelation has its impressive and authoritative lesson for the development of Christian truth, which is a continuous growth into the knowledge of Christ. The analogy of the old growth to the new is complete, and has the assurance of being God's method, which changes not. As the law of Moses expanded in significance and fulness through the spiritual insight of the prophets applying and elucidating it in relation to the problems of their times, so the comprehension of Christian truth is destined to grow from more to more "until we all come in the knowledge of the Son of God to the measure of the stature of the fulness of Christ." He of whose fulness we have all received relegated (as illustrated in the vision of transfiguration on the mount) Moses the lawgiver and Elijah the prophet, supreme in their day, to the realm of the subordinate and relative; a position their contemporary followers could not have conceived possible. Those also who own His supreme lordship and mastership are and must ever be striving to comprehend the height and depth and length and breadth of that which passeth knowledge, and to come into that larger and fuller possession of his mind which relatively dwarfs the conceptions even of the greatest men who have gone before us.

The growth of Christian knowledge is not a growth beyond Christ or apart from him, but into him. Christ being what he is, that growth cannot be other than limitless. As in him dwelt all the fulness of the Godhead bodily, it follows that in the highest reach of intellect and expression man is to count not himself to have apprehended, but to follow after if that he may apprehend. He is to hear the cheer of the Master's voice ever saying, "Ye shall see greater things than these." He is stimulated to deeper search for the unsearchable riches of that Master's mind and meaning by the promised guidance by his Spirit into all truth. But he cannot regard as all truth the fragments other men or ages have gained, however valuable and important, for it is the all-truth, not of the limited and imperfect minds who have sought, but of the All-perfect and the All-fair whom they sought. We see in our own age men rejoicing in the truth which an age previous could not discover since it could not bear, and find that increasing knowledge brings also increasing capacity to know; that its advance is from strength to strength, and from glory to glory. The progress of moral perception is too patent to be denied. The attitude of the whole

Christian world towards slavery, for instance, is other and far higher than it was for ages in the Christian Church. The vast provision and care for the sick in hospitals, for the weak-minded, as for the insane, for the reformation of criminals and the sanitary and decent housing of the poor; this whole humanitarian development which so strongly marks our century is not only a progress and advance in practical Christianity, but is a direct outcome of an enlarged and deeper vision of the humanity of Christ and of its meaning for the world. "Ecce homo!" is the cry which has led the Christian world into nobler practice than it ever attained in any earlier age. The old controversies and decrees concerning the metaphysical relations of the Divine and human in Christ, which found expression through the earlier Councils, these had their value for a speculative age and form to-day an intellectual basis for the more practical thought of our time. The realization and amplification of that truth, however, as it has sunk into the life and consciousness of men has deeply stirred and modified the life and manners of our age. It has turned the assertion of the Divine right of kings into the demand for the Divine rights of the people. That wonderful change in the conception of government which has swept over all Western Europe in our century, which holds no longer that the nation is for the ruler, but, whether under the republican or monarchical form, that the government is for the nation, this assertion of the democratic principle has come of profound conviction of the value and capacity of man as evoked by a larger and nobler conception of the Incarnation of the Son of God, who is the Son of Man.

It is plain to see that there are yet waiting large departments of Christian truth which promise rich fruitage for Christian knowledge and Christian life when once developed by the enlarged Christian experience of that ancient Church, which is the church of to-day and not the infant Church of the earlier centuries. One such sphere is the doctrine of God the Holy Ghost, the Lord and Giver of Life, a department of Christian doctrine which has heretofore had but scant notice from theologians even though under the dispensation of the Holy

Ghost the life of the world to-day is specially ordered of God. The visible presence of the Divine Son of Man is withdrawn, that the reign of his Spirit may begin and extend in power, that greater works may be done by Christ, through the Spirit, "according to the power which worketh in us," than were possible while the limitations of his mortal nature lay about him. How vast that range of knowledge opened by the Spirit which searcheth the deep things of God! which stretches on until the earthly and the heavenly seem to melt into one horizon and join together the earth and the sky, man's dwelling place and the source of spiritual light and life. What radiance may we not expect the developed doctrine of the Holy Ghost to throw on both the Church and the world, on worship in spirit and in truth, its services, its sermons, and its sacraments, and on the life of the Spirit in the truth, as it touches the vast and complex problems of our human intercourse and human destiny.

Some may naturally ask, What, amid all this expectant development of Christian truth, becomes of the faith once, or once for all, delivered to the saints? Yet one might as well ask of Science, what, amid all your fresh enlightenment, your law of gravitation (unknown to the fathers), and your heliocentric solar system, destructive of ancient postulates and forms of speech, your new chemistry and biology and geology; what amid all these becomes of the universe made once for all and as we formerly fancied in six terrestrial days? And the answer is the same in both cases. The cosmos was evoked from chaos once for all, and in it existed all that now exists, either as present reality or prospective certainty. No new law has been interposed and if new forms appear they were germinant there from the beginning. Science has not added a jot or tittle to the universe, but only something to the knowledge of it. It has simply educed and explained its ancient treasures. It brings in a new creation only in the sense of elucidating the old creation. Gravitation reigned before Newton, and evolution was going on amid the star dust æons before Darwin studied his pigeons. Copernicus did not disturb the sweet influences of the Pleiades recognized in Job's day; he merely expanded the single note of one constellation into the larger chorus of the illimitable heavens. And yet, though the law and the fact were there of old, who does not own the mighty power for good, through this great unfolding of them, in the elevation of man's thought, in the expansion of his spirit, in his awe of the mighty fabric in which he dwells, in his reverence for the order and truth and wisdom and beauty inherent in the Eternal Mind from which it all proceeds?

So it is of the faith once delivered. It is all contained, every atom, in Him, who is the sacred object of it. But as has been so well said by Professor Du Bose:

"If Jesus Christ is what the Church believes Him to be, He is and always will be very much more in Himself than our science of Him. Christology will, therefore, never be complete; but it is quite enough to convince us that there is a truth in it of which, while it is greater than our knowledge, we may yet know more and more. No human mind can grasp the unity or organic whole of nature, yet science knows that nature is such a whole, and that it can forever approximate to it. So the Church knows that Jesus Christ stands to us for a fact of God in nature and in humanity, of which it may know the truth, although it can forever only approximate to the whole truth."

Was there no gain for Christendom when St. John and St. James disclosed and developed the one its subjective principle and the other its objective law; no gain when St. Paul, by the force of his great genius, fit vehicle for so divine an inspiration, transformed the conception of Christ's Kingdom from that of an advanced Jewish sect into that of a Catholic Church; no gain when the great representative of a Christianized circumcision in his Epistle established as its rule the universal moral law instead of the ancient prescriptive ritual?

Did the Fathers at Nicæa add nothing to the stability of Christian progress, when they evolved, out of the facts long known and lived by, that stately confession hymn, the Nicene Creed? Think as a sober Christian of the confusion and perversion which would doubtless have come into Christendom had not their voice attuned itself in a new but accordant strain to the voice of the Gospel, not adding thereto but evoking therefrom the true key note of all the after progression. Has there come no gain to Christian thought and Christian life, no invigoration of its mental and moral atmosphere, from that clearer and nobler and deeper apprehension of the Atonement, which has been evolved through long periods of devout study? Whatever may be determined by any as to the particular content of the doctrine, now, at least, the aspect of the fact is changed from that of an ingenious and exceptional plan to meet a special exigency of the race into the revelation of an eternal element of God's nature, an element which manifests itself in all his rule of moral and spiritual beings, the deep and sacred element revealed in that law of sacrifice from which he does not hold himself exempt. Thus construed the Atonement makes Christ hanging on the cross, as well as standing before the empty tomb, the very revelation of God, in the deep things of whose being, the Christ is seen as the Lamb slain from the foundation of the world. To remove this great doctrinal fact from the realm of the abnormal, the transient, and the temporal into the realm of the unseen and the eternal is a gain for the intellect, for the conscience, and for the heart of man. The Atonement may well evoke a more vital and heartfelt response to its appeal when it is held, not as a perplexing enigma of celestial philosophy which bewilders and baffles us, but as the fulfilment in perfect completeness of the law which God out of his own nature has inlaid in our constitution; which is regnant in all noble life as it reflects God's life and is sacred to all deep affection which echoes his love; which making Christ really ours, makes God really ours, in that as we are Christ's, so Christ is God's.

We may fitly close this chapter by a passage from the writings of Dr. Philip Schaff.

"It is proper then to speak of progress in the Church itself. But this progress is never in the true sense creative, but comes only in the way of reception, organic assimilation, and expansion. All historical development in the Church consists in a cumulative apprehension of the life and doctrine of Christ and of his Apostles, and a progressive and ever increasing appropriation and manifestation of their spirit and method."

CHAPTER VI

THE CHRISTIAN LIFE AS SALVATION

IF progress in the apprehension of the truth is so essential, what becomes, it may be asked, of the truth essential to salvation if it needs must be a growing and expanding truth. Christ came to save men, and was there not enough truth to save men in the beginning, and if so what is the use of more? The answer is patent. Salvation is accord with God, and to come into accord with God is not simply to know, but to assimilate and come into harmony with what we know. The instrument of salvation is faith, the faith which is not chiefly intellectual assent but moral surrender, the committing of one's soul and life to the truth of God, the knowledge of which it possesses. Thus to believe Christ as he is revealed to us by coming unto him for rest, and taking his yoke upon us to guide our labor into rest, i. e.

by moral and spiritual surrender, this is for every soul salvation. But as we know more and learn more of Him, fuller surrender still is possible and also imperative for that accord with God, which is salvation. So St. Paul evidently felt when he spoke of leaving the things which are behind and pressing forward towards the mark for the prize of the high calling of God in Christ Jesus. He had had a knowledge of Christ very real, very consolatory, very stimulating; but he came in the course of his growth into the knowledge of Christ to feel that his previous knowledge had been a knowing of Christ after the flesh, from outside, as it were. But much as that knowledge had done for him, it could not satisfy him longer. Now henceforth know we him no more after the flesh, he exclaimed, but in the fuller truth of experience, and thought, and service, which had revealed him yet more completely; in the enlarged apprehension of his fulness which was ever growing, so that now his salvation was nearer and greater than when he first believed.

The completeness of man's salvation demands the intelligent reception of the truth, and a growth into the intelligent reception of it. All Christ's similes of the Christian life are similes of growth, of the growth of the building to completion, of the body to perfect harmony and health, of the leaven which spreads through all the lump, of the seed which expands into the wide branching tree, or from a handful multiplies into the harvest. But there are those who speak of the deposit of the faith as of the deposit of a certain sum in a bank, to be kept intact in some ancient napkin and not put out to increase. They talk of the truth that is to be believed, as though it were a certain definite amount of statement which could be weighed in the intellectual balance of one age, or measured by the definite doctrinal standard of one special time. The various Confessions so called of the various churches of the Reformation and the Decrees of the Council of Trent as a reply to them, are so many attempts thus to define and measure truth for their time, doubtless their authors thought for all time. But the places that knew them know them no more. How are these carefully elaborated statements outgrown, so that they must be explained even to explaining them away in order to hold on to them, and what sane man or church would essay such a task to-day? How different are these exclusive and excluding statements, seeking to limit the action of our Christian intellect within the bounds of a special confession, from those wonderful inclusive statements we call the Catholic Creeds, not into which we look, but through which we look up to God; which give us the great data of revelation, and leave the fulness of the apprehension of them to that growth in the mind of the Spirit which comes of experience according to the measure of the gift of Christ. Well may the Christian lips sing *Sursum Corda* as the Christian mind recognizes in Christ the light of the world, shining into every realm of his creation, that his disciples may follow him there as children of the light and of the day.

In thus recognizing the note of intelligence in the normal Christian life, evoked by the sound of the English tongue as the order of the Common Prayer begins, we but anticipate the lesson indicated in every service which the book contains. Let us but glance at the contents of this book, and at once we are struck with the presence of exhortation and explanation in all its services. The Daily morning and evening Prayer, after the scriptural call to God's presence, begin with the exhortation to the people setting forth the nature of the worship in which they are to engage. However tedious and cumbersome this daily iteration of what has been stigmatized as the little preachment may have come to be during the centuries in which intelligence has spread, and the leaven of the Prayer Book has raised the whole tone of reasonable worship in the Church, and however wise the action of our revisers in making the use of it optional, save on Sunday morning, still its presence in the early age of the Reformation was a distinctive feature witnessing both to the necessity of enlightening the mass of the people, whose worship in an unknown tongue had taken on largely the character of an incantation, and to its conception of true worship as an intelligent act of intelligent beings. Let these exhortations stand, though their use may be wisely curtailed, stand as monuments to witness to the Church's imprimatur on worship as a reasonable service, and on life as a life led in reason as in faith.

This feature of explanatory exhortation attends, as we have said, all the specially great services of the Book of Common Prayer. Baptism, Confirmation, the Administration of the Holy Communion, all share this feature in common with the order for Daily morning and evening Prayer. And even the more individual services, such as that of Holy Matrimony, and the private services, such as the visitation of the sick, and of prisoners, share this feature. Everywhere and in every place worshippers are to know what they are about. The *opus operatum* theory is not that on which these offices of worship are constructed. The subjective as well as the objective element must be present. There must be the individual response as well as the declared truth, the actual reception as well as positive donation of the grace. The analogy of nature, — since nature is God's ordinance and revelation in matter, — serves in the realm of the spirit. As there is no sound without the ear's auditory nerve receiving and conveying the vibrations of aerial movement to the brain; as sight is the eye's report back of the message of the sun's rays; as in fine there is no sensation, in all the assault of nature on the senses, until the senses have actively responded to the assault, so in the realm of spirit, the effect of truth and grace is conditioned by the reception it obtains. Truth and grace are indeed not created by man's response to them; they are forever the objective realities of God. Independent of man's recognition, they abide from everlasting in the bosom of the Eternal. But their power over life and character is conditioned by the soul's response. Holiness, purity, righteousness, worldliness, uncleanness, injustice; these come as man relates himself in harmony or in opposition to the objective truth and grace of God. Jangle all the bells in Christendom, and there is no sound for all the tumultuous leaping of the air, unless, entering the winding labyrinth of the single ear, the motion comes in touch with the living action of the brain, which answers to it. Proclaim in sermon, or offer in sacrament in clearest measure the living law of the Gospel, and without the soul's consent it leaves the soul impoverished still. Thus it is that the apprehension of the truth and the recognition of God's grace are so essential to vital worship and to the normal Christian life which it seeks to sanctify as God's in all its ways. Eternal life is God's gift, participation in it requires man's act of recognition and response.

Let us note, however, that this hortatory and explanatory feature of the Book of Common Prayer, inserted to secure an intelligent apprehension of its worship, is not an attempt to deny or dissipate the mystery of the spiritual life, or of the Being or the influence of the Eternal Spirit. It presupposes the reasonableness of prayer when it indicates its proper form, but it does not exploit its mystery. How our thoughts in worship reach the Eternal Mind, how our words in worship enter the Eternal Ear, and how the answer comes, these things must be left for the day when "we shall know even as we are known." The peace which proceeds of worship is a peace which passeth understanding. Were it not so it would be unreal, for it is the mystery of life reposing in the mystery of godliness. It is the unutterable yearning of the soul which cannot comprehend itself to find rest and strength and life in one who comprehends it, but whom it cannot comprehend. It is the outcome of

> " .... those obstinate questionings
> Of sense and outward things,
> Fallings from us, vanishings;
> Blank misgivings of a Creature
> Moving about in worlds not realized,
> High instincts before which our mortal Nature
> Doth tremble like a guilty Thing surprised . . .
> Which be they what they may,
> Are yet the fountain light of all our day,
> Are yet a master light of all our seeing;
> Uphold us, cherish, and have power to make
> Our noisy years seem moments in the being
> Of the eternal Silence."

In this mystery of prayer, and of salvation through its holy communion, "Deep calleth unto deep." It were a shallow thought indeed to think to explain away its mystery. But it is a noble thought to unfold that mystery as the reasonable refuge of the mystery of life and being. And so of the mysteries of the sacraments which body forth the mystery of the soul's birth from above, and of its nourishment by the very life and being of its Lord. The law of the soul's response finds sovereignty here, as elsewhere in the realm of the spirit, a response not creative but receptive of God's grace. The exhortation stands for an intelligent participation in the act that there may be an active coöperation, and so an efficacy of that which is symbolized in the washing of water and the partaking of the bread and wine. But who may explain the action? He only who can comprehend the soul, in its origin, its nature, and its destiny. Not he who is enwrapped all about with its mystery, who feels the need of heavenly things, and reaches out towards them, and believes he receives their benefit, but who, while realizing the effect, can no more explain the method of its impartation than he can understand how his thought is connected with the movement of his brain, though he accepts that connection, or explain how his arm moves at the motion of his mind, though he daily, hourly, nay every moment, is aware that muscle and nerve are obedient to the mandate of his will. As was long ago well said by Schleiermacher, "To clear up is not to clear out." We leave untouched the content of mystery in worship and in life. Thus only we fulfil their high behest, for in their nature they are mysteries, high, we cannot attain unto them. But for the conduct both of life and worship we seek the light of intelligence and reason, that their mystery may beckon and not baffle us. For, like the heavenly bodies in space, these spiritual realities abide, but we may approach them with the calm reverence of the astronomer or with the heated fancy of the astrologer. The latter gazes on the stars to turn their mystery into the mystification of portents, which reflect his own grotesque and wayward dreams, and give birth to omens both of delusive hopes and irrational fears. But the astronomer gazes upward, with the reverent homage of intelligent research, to learn what the stars teach him, and marking their orbit, motion, order, transforms what shines so far above him in the unfathomable mystery of space into a sure and certain guide for his pathway on the earth.

CHAPTER VII

THE CHRISTIAN LIFE AS INFLUENCED BY THE HOLY SCRIPTURES

WE have indicated the character of the Christian Life as one of Divine purpose and communion, of brotherly interest and ministration, of intelligent thought and investigation, both in the region of nature and in the realm of spirit. These features have been suggested by the contemplation of the Christian life as a life of Prayer, of common Prayer, of common Prayer in the common tongue of the living worshipper. We will proceed now to scrutinize more minutely the elements which constitute the substance of the Ritual. The permanence and progress of the Christian Life, its oneness with the past, its connection with the present, and its anticipative hold upon the future, are all suggested by the association of the worship with these three things: the Holy Scriptures, or sacred literature of past ages; the Collects, or the devout utterance of past ages; and the Christian Year, or religious sequence of worship recalling past ages. These features are fundamental in the Prayer Book, their correlated truths are fundamental in the normal Christian life.

Nothing is more striking than the association of English worship with the Bible. Its call to worship in the opening sentences of the Daily Prayer is resonant with the voice of the Prophets and Apostles of olden time. God's word, not man's, strikes the key note of its devotions. Whether as exhortation, or promise, or invitation, each Scripture sentence brings with it the aroma of an ancient association to mingle with the atmosphere of present worship; it is a sacred oracle attuned to the strain and stress of the spiritual want of to-day. And as the worship opens, so it continues. It is throughout simply saturated with the Scriptures. Its opening and invitatory burst of praise is an old psalm of the sanctuary and the synagogue. From this it turns to the Psalter, so rich in its record of spiritual experience that every mood of the religious life in all time finds expression in it, from the Alleluia of its joy to the De profundis of its sorrow and desolation. When David was supposed to have, as an author, almost a monopoly of the Psalter, Edward Irving, that Jeremy Taylor of Scotch divines, wrote of him, "His soul was like a harp full-stringed over which the angels of joy and sorrow swept as they passed, and which vibrated to every touch of human want or emotion." Our own Bishop Lay, in his homely and quaint prose, used to say of it, "The reading of the Psalter is for the Episcopalian what the experience or class meeting is for the Methodist, only with the personal pronoun I subdued or left out altogether." Then the lessons from the Old and New Covenant come on, holding up ancient history as a mirror of modern motives, and proclaiming the same Law and Gospel to be regnant in the time immediately present as in times far past. Each special service has its special scripture. In Baptism we read from the Gospel of Christ's treatment of children as the plea that "he favorably alloweth this charitable work of ours in bringing this infant to his Holy Baptism." Confirmation has its lesson concerning the laying on of the Apostles' hands. The Holy Communion not only stations the Law given by Moses at its gate, but in its Epistle and Gospel provides the grace and truth which came by Jesus Christ for the comfort and instruction of the soul which has passed through the gate into the streets of the city to sit down at meat with the Master. If the Marriage Service does not contain a Gospel, it refers to it in its fine phrase concerning the holy estate which " Christ adorned and beautified with his presence and the first miracle that he wrought in Cana of Galilee," and associates it with the Epistles quoting the commendation of St. Paul concerning the honorableness of marriage in all men. The Burial Service is ushered in with the old Testament's anticipation of triumph and consolation, and is alive with the voice of Angels proclaiming the risen Lord, who is affirmed to be the pledge of our immortality in the glowing argument of the Apostle Paul.

Thus all life from the cradle to the grave is wrought about with Scripture. And what is the meaning of it, if not this, that there is a permanence of the normal religious life which to be profound and true may, nay must, draw an inspiration from the past, wherein men lived and wrought and suffered under God as we, and yet whose past looked inevitably on to our present, "God having provided some better thing for us, that they without us should not be made perfect." It is not the purpose here to draw out a doctrine of Holy Scripture, either from the Article which makes it a final arbiter of doctrine, or from the liturgical affirmation concerning it as the oracles of God. It is patent from the use of it that the Church in its Prayer Book holds that God in times past spake unto the fathers by the Prophets, and hath spoken unto us by his Son, and that that voice rightly understood is the supreme spiritual authority and guide. Theories of inspiration, or composition, or compilation, these fortunately are not found in any part of the Prayer Book, for their place is in the outer court of criticism, and not in the inner court of the sanctuary where men ought to worship. These come and go as men learn or unlearn, as the new light dawns, or the old light glows afresh. But worship is the continuous attitude of man towards God, not towards the servants of his will, even the holiest of them. What the "sundry times and divers manners" in which He spake through men involve, will evolve in his providence as like the commended Bereans we search the Scriptures, or like the prophets themselves search diligently what or what manner of time the spirit of Christ which was in them did signify, "unto whom it was revealed that not unto themselves but unto us they did minister."

But the constant quality of Scripture lies not in the realm we label "Introduction," in names, dates, sequences, and what not of the outer form, but in that inner core of life and living truth which is profitable for instruction in righteousness; in that Divine quality which quickens the spirit by its inspiring force; in that practical efficiency which can fashion the use of Divine truth in all things unto edification, so that the man of God may be perfect, thoroughly furnished unto all good works. Now the liturgical use of Holy Writ makes manifest this quality of the Scriptures, and applies it in many salutary ways. First of all it gives the sense of the permanence of the Divine Presence in the life of humanity in all its changeable estate; then the assurance of the ineradicable possession by humanity of the religious instinct which recognizes God's presence, and then the conviction of the universal necessity of the development of the religious life, which incorporates God's truth, for the development of the worthiest life of men. This on the conservative side. And on the progressive side, the liturgical use of the Scripture as fully shows that the very nature of the religious life is such that it is a growth up into God; that both the unfolding capacity of man and the unfailing fulness of God require and involve the ever increasing apprehension and enlarged application of divine truth on the part of men, the progress, in fine, of humanity into a fuller life in God.

Thus the lesson of the Scriptures for the present age is one of hope, of widening scope, of higher achievement, than all the past can show. By the liturgical use of the Holy Scriptures in its daily worship, the soul is brought face to face with both the permanent and progressive elements of the religious life; its claim on his reverent faith in the past and the vindication of its practical hold on the things of the present. And it does all this by simply unfolding to the mind what religion has been in the world and how it has been. History has been well said to be "philosophy teaching by example," and the Bible may be as truly said to be "theology taught by life." For in the Bible, its narratives, its poems, its prophecies, its histories, and its letters, we learn at once of religion as a concrete reality. We find, from the very way in which its messages come to us, that God's revelation to men was a ruling of them. He came down into life, the life of Abraham the individual, of Israel the race, not first of all into a literature through a book full formed.

That was the conception of Mohammed as presented in the Koran, and of Joseph Smith in his Mormon Bible. They professed to receive these long literary compositions direct from heaven, and these they presented as the revelation of the Divine will and as the law of the Divine life. To them revelation came in the form of a composition. To the Hebrew it was recognized as a communication to the soul and life. Therefore the Hebrew and the Christian Scriptures are not like these later Bibles of the Mohammedans and Mormons; they are not compositions about a life antecedent to its actual realization, but are the literary outcome of a life already lived or being lived in the recognition of God, who had already revealed himself to that life and inspired it. Revelation to them was not in the letter, but in the spirit. Its method was not the dictation of a book, but the inauguration of a life, whose origin, movement, growth, the Book records, and out of which, filled with the same inspiring spirit as the life, we draw our instruction and inspiration as from the life itself.

To be confronted with the Scriptures then in worship is to be brought face to face with the life of the race in God from the beginning. It is to be made to recognize the everlasting purpose of God to bring men to their highest self by bringing them to Himself. It is to be brought into touch with the vitality of the religious life we ourselves are seeking as evidenced in every stage of man's progress, and to learn the doctrine of God and of man's relation to him, not so much by dogmatic statement, or philosophical speculation, as by a contemplation of the life of a people consciously led by him; led by him through all the centuries as well as through the wilderness, "to prove them and know what was in their heart, whether they would keep his commandment or no," who "humbled them and suffered them to hunger and fed them with manna, that he might make them know that man doth not live by bread only, but that by every word that proceedeth out of the mouth of the Lord doth man live."

The atmosphere of a worship thus replete with Scripture is one which breathes vitality and reality into religious living; the vitality and reality of the life of God in the life of humanity. It discriminates religion from the region of heated fancy and hysteric feeling, as breathing the free air of genuine life and struggle. It dissipates the doubt that religion may be a passing phase of man's development, as Auguste Comte affirmed, proper enough, nay, inevitable in the childhood of the race, but to be put away with childish things as the grown man enters the realm of thought and knowledge and reasonable action. Through the Scripture the assurance is confirmed that that life cannot be ephemeral in its fundamental elements which has filled past ages with its power; that that cannot be a mere individual sentiment which has proved the strength of a great and beyond measure influential civilization. And thus the historic continuity of religion, recorded as it was enacted in the pages of the Bible, brings with it the conviction of an everlasting purpose of God to bring mankind into living and loving relation to himself, the recognition and acceptance of which purpose by man constitutes his religious life. This affirmation of the soul, so strong and abiding, so salutary and so inspiring, vindicates itself as distinct from delusion by the fact of its long illustration in the history of mankind. Thus the single soul, the man of modern times, we of to-day, gain the assurance which is a natural deduction from past experience, that in our moral and spiritual endeavor we are not helpless strugglers against the world and the universal trend of things, but are co-workers together with God, the unfolding of whose purpose the Bible portrays.

The spirit we receive out of the Scriptures is one of confidence; "not the spirit of fear but of power, of love, and of a sound mind."

The very imperfections and crudities attending the historical progress of religion; the depravities and cruelties mingled with it, as seen depicted in this honest and almost naive chronicle of Holy Writ ; these do not witness against the reality or worth of religion, but for its persistent power and for God's unfaltering purpose to evolve a moral and spiritual life for mankind out of and in the midst of the most untoward circumstances. Ignorance, stubbornness, moral blindness, abominable idolatries, and debasing sensualities pressed in upon it and ofttimes perverted it. We see it in these pages as a light shining in the darkness, which comprehended it not; but the light though obscured never went out. The sign and witness of the power of religion were just these continual conflicts, this unceasing confrontment of evil, with the rebuke of God; this brooding of the Spirit of God over the moral chaos and the projection of a moral cosmos out of it. It did not come at first in perfect form, unstained, unmarred, but was ever a growing power of moral order as the mind grew in spiritual enlightenment and the conscience cleared under the discipline of God's providence. We may wonder that the author of the Epistle to the Hebrews could refer to Gideon and Barak and Samson and Jephthah as heroes of faith, and they would indeed prove sorry samples of sainthood seen by the after light; but with all their faults it was their faith in God which ennobled their lives above their fellows, and rendered possible as their successors in the leading of the nation such heroes as Samuel, David, and the Prophets.

The final outcome of all this history, seen as we turn from the Old Testament to the New, is the crowning vindication of both the permanence and the progress of the religious instinct guided and moulded by the hand of God. For of Israel according to the flesh came Christ Jesus, a name confessedly above every name in the moral and spiritual realm, a name to which all bow in that reverence of supreme deference to absolute righteousness, which no force of will can repress even when the reverence of obedience is withheld. It is not irreverent to say that Christ came not unconnected with the past. His life was not projected into the life of the race by a sudden Divine fiat, all unrelated to the life which had preceded him. It was only " in the fulness of the times" that God sent forth his Son into the world. He was the culmination of the everlasting purpose of God, which had been manifest in all that had gone before. He is the crown of humanity, as he is the earthly image of the invisible God; the Son of Man, the Son of God; the one in whom the law of God was transfigured into the life of God, and in whom love, which underlies the law and is the life, reveals itself as sacrifice. He comes to us in the Gospels as one bearing the burdens of humanity and engaged in all its activities; a very real personage, who lived and taught and suffered; not exempt from the laws pertaining to humanity, not apart from its infirmities, but still the perfect fulfilment of all God's thought concerning it. And this one, so matchless in character, so boundless in devotion to his fellow men, whose thought still penetrates the world and elevates its spirit to regions before unknown and not yet attained; He, the exhaustive illustration of the law of sacrifice in man's relation to his fellow men, whose word passeth not away, but which speaks with authority to the mind and conscience of this century, this one based all his doctrine of man and all claim to their spiritual allegiance on the assurance that God spake in him and that his being was one with the Father. He knew man and what was in man so well that his word concerning him, his being, his relations, his destiny, is recognized as the supreme word, as the word still regnant in modern civilization.

He who knew man so well has the witness that he knew his own manhood too, its nature, its secret source of power, its spiritual relationship, its destiny. And that was all affirmed to be in God, that was all depicted as the fulfilment of a divine purpose which was from eternity, a plan which affirms that man's relation to God and his service to him is the ultimate purpose of his being, and vindicates religion, which is man's recognition and response to God's purpose, as the supreme and abiding element of life. Other elements may lie latent in some or be obstructed and seem altogether absent in others, as the faculty of art, or of science, or of philosophical speculation, which represent the mind as related to special departments of the manifold life of the spirit. But this direct relation to the Author of life, this supreme relation of religion, is the one which is universal, which is permanent, and which is the root of progress in all that most ennobles and distinguishes humanity.

Thus to be brought in worship constantly face to face with the Scripture concerning Christ is to gain the sense of that supreme stability and absolute worth in religion which makes it man's one secure possession. Tracing in the older Scripture the religious struggle and growth of man up to Christ, and in the newer the life and enthusiasm and joyous confidence of men believing in and inspired by Him, this brings the assurance of a growth and development of spiritual power through all its changes, which stamps it as a divine reality, which the world can never give nor take away. For, as Dean Stanley so well said, "It is the transitory which stands still and fades and falls to pieces; the eternal continues by changing its form in accordance with the movement of advancing ages." The Scriptures in fine breathe an atmosphere in which martyrs and confessors may well be bred, as they have been bred; the atmosphere of a stalwart manhood and of a quenchless enthusiasm. And this is the characteristic which the Scriptural quality of the Prayer Book's worship engenders in its revelation both of the permanence and progress of the spiritual life of men.

CHAPTER VIII

THE BEARING OF THE COLLECTS ON THE CHRISTIAN LIFE

IN the devotional use of the Collects of the ages, as given in the Prayer Book, the worshipper voices his prayers and praises in the language of other men and other times. No objection need lie against such worship as archaic and artificial, as a crass conservatism which cramps worship by restricting its expression to an ancient formula, and by depreciating the utterance of present wants in the language of the present hour. For the fundamental wants of human nature and the essential adoration of the heart are the same in all ages. What has once expressed them well has capacity still to utter them. Common worship can only voice the fundamental and, because fundamental, the common wants of men. The special exigency of each individual must find its expression in the closet. "The heart knoweth its own bitterness, and the stranger intermeddleth not with its joy." In the congregation we must express what we share in common, one with another. If ours is to be common worship, not individualistic, a common form must fashion it. It cannot depend on any one man's mood, nor express itself through any one man's interpretation. The demand of common worship is for common utterance. Now what common utterance can promise so much completeness as that which is common, not merely to one community or to one age, but which is replete with the aspiration and supplication of all the ages; which is not a modern manufacture but an ancient growth; which condenses into itself the sighing and singing of hearts long since at rest, together with the exultations and the plaints of those still compassed about with the trials and the joys of this present time? This is the usage of the Book of Common Prayer.

There was temptation enough at the time of its formation to cut off altogether from past usages which had been so overladen with abuse. But the liturgical instinct was keen and subtle enough to respond to the vibrant touch and living association of the old forms of devotion. The Reformers did not think they were cutting themselves off from the true life of the past. They were reaffirming it rather by their excision of so much cumbrous and illegitimate overgrowth, which hid the form and perverted the spirit of that past. They felt the more drawn to the heroes of the age of primitive simplicity, in that they were striving to restore that primitive simplicity. They would not make or declare themselves ecclesiastical orphans by rejection of the Fathers. The fires of devotion which burned anew in them leaped in response to the enkindling devotions of the olden time. Thus out of that past they drew those matchless forms and set them to our lips, so that, with hearts attuned to the same sanctity of desire, the mouth might speak with the same melody of utterance.

We cannot here enter into any examination of the wonderful beauty, dignity, serenity, spirituality, of these ancient Collects. Each utters its own separate note, yet all combine, through the unity of the Christian year, into a rich harmony of rounded Christian experience. But the chief value for us of the use of these matchless forms lies not in their pervasive beauty and order, though these invest the Christian life with a sense of its completeness and elevation, which suggest its refinement of tone as well as its strength of character. It lies in the impression of the permanence and progress of a Christian experience which comes inevitably, if unconsciously, from using as our own the forms which framed the petitions of the bygone saints of old. With the Lord's Prayer falling from the Master's lips as the key note, the stately progression continues from age to age, from the days of St. Chrysostom to the times of the Reformation. For with the older Collects are mingled those now old to us, but new when the Prayer Book was compiled, namely, the comprehensive and sonorous "Prayer for all sorts and conditions of men," and the "General Thanksgiving" of Bishop Reynolds, which have vindicated by their fulness of meaning and beauty of expression their right to stand among the more ancient forms. But this use of the old forms, so apt in the expression of our own wants, intensifies the impressing of our unity with the Christian life of old. That life is ever individual, but not simply individual; it is a life of communion and fellowship with all saintly souls, or souls striving to be saintly. It is a practical realization of that communion of saints which we declare in the Creed to be an article of our belief. It brings in the sense of oneness with the vast throng whom no man can number, who have striven and suffered and been consoled as we; of that "one army of the living God," whose equipment and armament may have varied, but whose advance has been steadfast through all the changes of the centuries. It imparts a sense of kinship with the martyrs and confessors who have suffered for the faith; with the saints and the doctors who have adorned it with the resplendent light of learning and devotion; with the heroes who have stood for it amid all contending forces of pagan unbelief, or the tyranny of unrighteous ecclesiastical rule; with the vast multitude who in all ages have lived faithful and true lives in the following of their Lord, who indistinguishable from one another yet stand in their intermingled strength and sweetness like the milky way of the skies, a bridge of light leading to the celestial country. Yes, as the Christian worshipper to-day uses the same petitions which they of old time proffered, he gains a vivid sense of the power and reality of these prayers through the attesting lives of those who by their use gained strength, and feels himself conjoined by an indissoluble bond of unity to the whole family of God. For therein, as in the Scriptures, he finds witness again to the permanence of that life to which his own soul is so strongly moved, and holds on in increasing confidence to the reality of that faith and hope to sustain him, which has upheld through all the ages the highest life of men.

But not only do these Collects minister to the sense of permanence and oneness of the Christian life since the coming of the Christ. Its progress is not less suggested and assured. For these prayers have themselves come into being in the ever advancing stages of that life, and themselves form a progression in worship as in life. It was aptly said by that lofty religious genius, the matchless Phillips Brooks, that "the only way to get rid of a past is to make a future of it." And we may say as truly, that the only way to really gain a past and make it ours, is to grasp its life so as to reproduce it in forms fitted to our time and circumstances. It must not remain to us simply a bygone thing of wonder and admiration, with which we have no vital connection, like an Egyptian pyramid, or a cave dwelling in a cliff. These belong to a civilization with which we have nothing in common, from which we can gain no impulse, to which we turn only in curiosity, as we turn to a fossil form embedded in the rocks. The past becomes ours only as it vivifies our life. It is real to us not as a mere accumulation of material deposited, a talent wrapped in a napkin as in a shroud. To be living to us, as it was to them of old time, it must be as the seed which reproduces a harvest, similar but not the same. So these ancient Collects make the past real to us, as they make the present real; their vitality as ancient witnesses depends on the vitality of their present ministration, in joining past and present together in one. They in worship perform the function so essential to the abiding permanence and progress of the Christian life, which is, to quote the felicitous phrase of Père Gratrey, "To speak the Word of God afresh to every age, in accordance with the novelty of the age, and the eternal antiquity of the truth."

CHAPTER IX

THE INFLUENCE OF THE CHRISTIAN YEAR ON THE CHRISTIAN LIFE

THE Christian year is that happy and indelible feature of the Common Prayer which adds its testimony to the value of the life which is ever new as it is ever old. As the Bible is witness to the permanence and progress of religion in all ages, as the Collects bear their testimony to the religious permanence and progress of all the Christian centuries, so this Christian year, tracing the footsteps of our Lord from Bethlehem's manger to the ascension from Olivet, is the attestation to the life and power of Him who is both the root and the offspring of David, the alpha and the omega, the beginning and the ending, which is and which was and which is to come, and to that life of his followers in Him, which if it be a permanent abiding in his love must be a continuous growth into his image.

It is in the devotional progress of the Christian year that the religious life is brought face to face with the Lord and Master of it; with the Christ which was of old that he might be formed anew in every believing heart. And that life as we trace its stages is seen and felt to be the ever expanding life, perfect at each stage, yet each stage a stage of perfection beyond that which preceded it. The life of the obedient boy passed beyond the abnegation of the passive infant life; the life of perfect service in the home to earthly parents budded into the recognition and acceptance of wider service in the ampler house of the Heavenly Father; the years of perfect labor in the workshop emerged through the temptation struggle of the wilderness into sterner struggle in the world's wilderness of sin; the perfect teaching and the perfect work (the parable and miracle of perfect devotion) deepened into the perfect obedience of suffering and the cross, wherein we find the culmination of the perfect sacrifice which runs through and consecrates every feature of that sacred life. We see the mount of exaltation rising from out the very edge of the valley of death's shadow. The "It is finished" of the earthly renunciation becomes the transition point to the sphere of heavenly dominion. The burial is the seed of resurrection, the perfect submission of the cross, the germ of perfect power on the throne. As we thus follow the steps of that most holy life, we find in it the highest illustration of spiritual permanence and progress; ever full life in God, ever the expanding power of that life. And thus the Master becomes all our own. His word transforms God's general law into a direct personal appeal, and witnesses to the divine calling of every portion of our life and to the inevitable progress of it, if it be life in him. It translates all its obligation into the realm of love, and suffuses the snowy purity of its divine morality with the warmth of personal affection and allegiance. Thus the religious life is made full as it is made personal, for, in the words of Tennyson, the poet prophet of our time, "Christianity with its divine morality, but without the central figure of Christ, the Son of Man, would become cold, and it is fatal for religion to lose its warmth."

Above all other aids to devotion in the Prayer Book the use of the Christian Year makes prominent this one distinctive feature of the Christian life. By it our gaze is centred on a person, and faith is disclosed as a living relation to him, and is not depicted as chiefly an acceptance of propositions about him, which is commonly styled acquiescence in dogma. Dogma has its rightful place. It is, like the science of any truth, a matter for the schools. The mathematical formulæ of the sun's motion, of the parallax of the stars, of the law of gravitation, are most valuable, nay, essential and inevitable, in giving us fixed laws of thought concerning them. But the sun's light and warmth are what we live by. It is basking in the sunlight, not the acceptance of or acquiescence in accurate formulæ of scientific precision concerning its nature and action, which sends the glow of life through our frames. Botany gives us the science of the earth's flora and clears our thought concerning it. But we live by the garden, not by the treatise upon it. These sciences do not add to or make potent the facts of which they treat. They only classify and explain them. And it is so with dogmatic theology. It is a mental clearance. It possesses the value of an accurate statement of Christian truths and of their relations. But to accept a dogma is not salvation. Salvation is to accept Him whom the dogma defines. The Prayer Book's conception, judged by its use, is not salvation by propositions, but salvation by Christ. Its baptismal requirement is not a confession, or philosophical explication of doctrine, but a creed, an acceptance of facts which bind the soul to a living person. And the Christian Year has for its object, not the instilling of a scheme of doctrine, but the vivid presentation of a living Lord, whom to know is life eternal, whom to love is bliss ineffable, "whom to serve is to reign."

The normal Christian life as indicated by the features of its worship just enumerated, viz. its Scriptural association, its use of the ancient Collects, and the following of the Christian Year, is thus portrayed as a life of assured reality as historically vindicated, of legitimate development as historically associated, of genuine vitality as rooted in the historic Christ.

It holds within it a sense of permanence, and a prophecy of progress, which strengthen and irradiate it with the illimitable hope which affirms, "The eternal years of God are hers." One who is a partaker of it does not wander in the realm of hectic dreams, does not follow illusive phantoms, does not chase elusive unrealities. He dwells in the secret place of the Most High. There is a calmness within which comes of a sense of permanent possession, and a vitality which indicates healthy conviction and enduring energy.

But for all this, one of the chief charges which is brought against religion to-day is, not that it has no value of restraint and guidance for the unthinking and ignorant, but that it is destined to pass as unvindicated to minds enlightened by the disclosures of knowledge and thought characteristic of this century. It has had, men say, its uses and abuses, but what renders it a creed outworn is that its postulates are not verifiable. It is an instrument of the past. Henceforth men will be guided by what they know, not by what they have believed. Much of the indifference to religion lurks in the suspicion that it dwells in the region of uncertainties.

It is an immense tribute to the value of the Book of Common Prayer that it generates a spirit the opposite of all this. It stands for the distinct credibility and reliability of the data on which its worship is based and by which its life is vindicated; not directly as it were, but rather presumptively, as involved in the devotional use of its historical documents. And the question arises, Is the Prayer Book justified in this use? Whatever it teaches, has it a right to teach that the religious element in mankind is a valid and fundamental characteristic, a permanent postulate of man's nature, and not a temporary form of his experience? Is it indeed, can it be shown to be, an expanding power conditioning man's noblest growth, because rooted in the profoundest depths of his being?

There is but one answer to this challenge from one nurtured in the use of the Book of Common Prayer. The religious element in man is as fundamental and pervasive as any other element of his nature. If catholicity or ubiquity of presence is a testimony to validity, it can stand confident in the presence of science, art, or literature. These, which seek at times to replace religion, are its children, and remind one of Lear's ungrateful daughters when they try to dethrone their parent. Are the results of these declared verifiable because an eclipse may be forecast, because the frame thrills at the touch of beauty, or the mind responds in consent to intellectual appeal? But has not religion its verification in its results? Was ever any vindication of the truth more triumphant than that given by the Person of the Master of our souls, when he claims to be the Truth? Does Christ make no convincing appeal to the heart or the intellect? Were eyes ever smitten with such a vision of loveliness as the soul by the image of Jesus of Nazareth? Has Christ's word no verification in the realms of human life which it has purified and sweetened, in the realms of thought it has cleared and elevated, in the regions of action it has made just and merciful and reasonable and strong? Christian civilization, with all its faults and crudities and unrealized possibilities, is, compared with any other civilization, a potent vindication of Christian truth. The Christian religion stands fearlessly before the Master's searching test, "by their fruits ye shall know them." The leavening power of that civilization has been the mind of Christ; the mind of Christ was the consummate flower of the long abiding of Israel under the shadow of the Almighty, when once touched by the light which streamed direct from heaven. And the fruitage of that mind, which dwelt in the secret place of the Most High, has been the spiritualization of life, the elevation of its ethical standard, the purification of its manners, the repression of its animalism, the ennobling of manhood, the elevation of womanhood, the amelioration of childhood. The vast expansion of sympathy, help, enlightenment, and kindly care which we call the humanitarian movement of our time, finds its root in Christ's life and word. No department of that life but the mind of Jesus has touched, and touching adorned, nay, rather expanded and glorified,

"As if they surely knew their sovran Lord was by."

And yet it is the judgment of sober reason

that in its effect upon social institutions and the intricate problems of human competition and co-operation that mind is not only unexhausted, but has scarcely begun to be felt and understood. The abolition of slavery may be regarded as but the prelude to that full freedom of mankind when once the Son shall have made it free, and it shall be free indeed. Therefore we say that the legitimacy of religion as a factor in man's life is verifiable. No fulfilment of scientific prophecy as of the real presence of an unseen planet, no building up of an unknown and extinct creation from a fragment of its bone, no vindication of scientific prediction, in fine, affords clearer evidence of the truth of its data and the soundness of its methods, than is furnished to religion by its salutary and ennobling influence on the individual, on society, on the state. "That which we have seen with our eyes, and which we have looked upon, and our hands have handled, of the word of life," in its effects, is potent verification of the divine reality, of that word seen, looked upon, and handled by the Apostles in its source, the person of the Christ.

In derogation of this claim, however, men are not slow to point to many evils which have been attendant on the development of religion and to some generated by it. The Inquisition, indeed, is not a lovely feature of Christian ecclesiasticism, nor the patronage of slavery in Christian times, nor the persecution of the Jews, nor the *auto-da-fé* of heretics. Superstition and fanaticism have all along beclouded the truth of Christianity, and worldliness and ambition have continually perverted its pathway. But the question is not whether religion sprang forth complete and purified in the beginning, not whether it has made no mistakes, and cherished no errors, and enforced no wrongs, but whether it has persisted with the vigor of an original force, until it has become more and more a power for good in the life of men. Neither art nor science can stand the test sought to be applied to the disparagement of religion. Astrology and alchemy once stood in the place now held by astronomy and chemistry. These were erratic movements in the course of scientific progress, which do not, however, throw doubt on the validity of science.

Something was gained even by their fanciful investigations for the science which emerged from their bewilderments and discarded them. Æsthetics form still a valid department of man's culture, for taste is a persistent element of human nature which cannot be extirpated, though its final decisions contradict and bar out the earlier dicta of its utterance. Angelo and Tintoret, Beethoven and Wagner, are still valid interpreters of beauty to sight and sound, though plastic art has developed from the war-paint of the Indian to the glow of Claude and Titian, and the tom-tom of the savage may have been the remote progenitor of the unfinished Symphony of Schumann. In fine, any valid endowment of human nature vindicates its permanent vitality by its power of survival over error, and by its growth through imperfection to perfect form. It is a strong and striking tribute to the presence of an eternal force within the Church that it contains this power of reformation and recuperation. Reformation is not something to be excused and apologized for, as though it were a blot, though a necessary blot, upon the fair fame of the

Church; is not to be regarded as an unlovely scar, a disfigurement of the sacred body, which it behooves us to hide as much as possible; a witness to wounds more than to healing power. No, just that act of recuperation from dire disease, which we call in the Church the Reformation, is the sacred witness to the power of divine life within it. Christ said, — I quote the pungent phrase, — "Christ said the Church should not die, but he did not say it should never be sick." And to come through enfeebling sickness to jocund health vindicates the inherent vitality of the frame. One might as well be apologetic for his renewed vigor after his recovery from the typhoid fever, which has purged his system of many noxious germs, as to be ashamed and to speak in bated breath, as of some family scandal, of that manifestation of germinant divine power in the Church which we call the Reformation. It is rather a strong proof of the permanence of the Church that it can "be transformed by the renewing of its mind."

But, once more, men say, that for all its early origin and persistent hold, for all the purifying power it shows in what we call the permanent relations of man's life, religion yet differs fatally from art and science in that its fundamental postulate is not knowledge, but faith, not conviction which comes of known fact, but assumption which arises from felt necessity. Its evidence is from the realm of the unseen, its substance is not of possession but of hope.

What then shall we say about the solid globe? Modern science reduces it to force, and the conflict or co-operation of forces. It too is the visible effect of an unseen power which we assume from a felt necessity, that is, if any coherence is to be found in nature, and any coherent reading of it, which we call science. To read it at all, man must assume things which he cannot prove, assume them from the felt necessity of the case; as, namely, the permanence of natural law, the faithful report of the senses to the brain, and the integrity and reliability of the action of our intellectual powers. These are the assumptions of science, in the realm of the unseen; not irrational but beyond the region of proof. They are an illustration of what the great Laureate said,

"All that is worth proving is beyond the power of proof." Religion does nothing more. It only acts in a different department of our being, in that which allies us with the unseen and eternal rather than with the visible and temporal. Man's spiritual nature is irrepressible, it is originant, persistent, expansive, manifest in its effects, and these of the highest worth. And it cannot be irrational to rest confident in the postulates it involves, of God, of man's spiritual nature, of ethical relation, of religious aspiration, seeing these are the inherent necessities for the explication of its phenomena which prove their validity by their worth. The one irrational conclusion would be to affirm that our consciousness is true in its deliverances concerning nature, and false in its deliverances concerning morals. If we distrust it as it speaks in conscience, we must distrust it as it speaks in reason. To sweep away as invalid the postulates of religion is to declare untrustworthy the postulates of science; is to bring in universal scepticism.

We hold then that religion, as taught and assumed in the Prayer Book, is a permanent possession of mankind, and that the religious life which it advocates is a life of unclouded rationality, of progressive power, of illimitable hope; it is secure, it is inalienable. It has the promise of the life which now is and of that which is to come. Its energies are called out in steadfast and enthusiastic action, for they are co-operative with God's purpose. Its aspiration after things honest, true, lovely, and of good report (in every realm of God's creation) is hopeful and courageous, for it is the fulfilment of God's plan. It is assured as it looks back, or around, or before, or above, for its call is to "the confidence of a certain faith," and to "the comfort of a reasonable, religious, and holy hope." It is not a negative denial of life's fulness, but a positive assertion of man's divine capacity to grow ever more and more both in the knowledge and manifestation of the truth. It is not hesitant, or apologetic, and cannot be ashamed. Its voice is a veritable *Sursum Corda*, whether it call to duty, to conflict, or to achievement, and the soul's true answer is, "I will lift up mine eyes unto the hills, from whence cometh my strength. My help cometh from the Lord, which made heaven and earth."

CHAPTER X

THE CHRISTIAN LIFE AS TAUGHT BY THE SACRAMENT OF BAPTISM

WE are now to look at the normal Christian life as taught by the sacraments, as they are ministered according to the Book of Common Prayer. About these sacraments the storm of controversy has raged, so that in entering their atmosphere it is difficult not to be engulfed in it. But on any theory the sacraments themselves witness to all men two great conceptions of life, viz. life begotten of God and life nourished by God. They bear their testimony to the vital connection of God's spirit and man's spirit. They indicate by their striking symbolism that the truly natural life is what we call the supernatural life, by which is meant that man's true nature joins him on to God, that the life which is of God must be man's life, or he falls short of the ideal of his life. In this normal Christian life, or the religious life in conformity to its law, Baptism stands for the initiation, and the Holy Communion for the perpetuation and development. What light they throw upon the normal Christian life, as they are conditioned and ministered by the ritual of the Prayer Book, we proceed now to inquire.

We look first at Baptism. And the first point which strikes us in relation to Baptism is its universality of intention. It is meant for all, men, women, and children; nor is it in the Prayer Book restricted to any special class of these. It is not limited to children of communicants. The special sin of neglect by father or mother does not furnish an impediment. Illegitimacy of nature does not banish from the legitimacy of the Kingdom. Baptism in its primal attitude stands for the universal grace of God; it declares a Divine Fatherhood which is not willing that any should perish. It proclaims that, as the redemption through Christ is for all, so his Kingdom, in which his life may be most completely and normally lived, is for all. By this symbolical witness and seal to the largeness of God's mercy and forgiveness, Baptism makes known that, in gaining this life from above, it is not man who first seeks God, but God who first seeks man. It teaches that man's attitude in regard to God's grace is not to create it or compel it, or to deserve it, to win it by penance or to wring its reluctant compliance by agony of argument and the soul's distress, but that his true attitude is simple acceptance of it. In redemption he grasps a hand already held out. The grace and help from above are the *prius* in man's spiritual life. "We love him because he first loved us." And this love which wrought the redemption in Jesus Christ is not repelled by any hereditary taint which we call original sin, — so called because it makes sin originant in each human soul engendered of Adam. Whatever according to the 9th Article that sinful trend may deserve, Baptism declares that it gets grace. And as Baptism in the case of infants precedes actual trangression, the application of this sacrament to them teaches that God's grace goes before (prevents) them as well as follows them, anticipates their desire as well as responds to it, is meant to preserve from transgression as well as to remit it; in fine, claims all children as God's children from the start. Thus the root of the normal religious life, as construed by Baptism, is consciousness of life as a vocation of God. It is a recognition of his voice calling to our earliest days, "Come up higher." It stands for the spirit of adoption by which we cry, Abba, Father. Hence it is evident that children are brought to Baptism not in the first instance to make God gracious to them, but because he is gracious to them. The Scripture from St. Mark's Gospel read in this service is a kind of *apologia pro gratia sua;* a vindication of this service of grace by reason of God's disposition of grace; a recognition of the truth that "of such is the Kingdom of Heaven," by initiating them into that Kingdom. The exhortation following this Scripture points out: "Ye perceive how by his outward gesture and deed he declared his good will towards them," — and declares further that we perform this act of Baptism because we are thus "persuaded of the good will of our Heavenly Father towards this infant." There could not be a stronger attestation of what men call the prevenieht grace of God than the Baptismal Service of the Book of Common Prayer. And this means that Christian ordinances do not create the grace they signify, but simply witness to it and apply it. They too are the outcome of the prevenient grace which establishes them as its witnesses and agents. They are called in ecclesiastical language seals, because they make valid, by a divinely ordered act, a general fact in a particular case. So that, whatever Baptism effects, it does not create the gracious disposition of God towards the recipient of it. It is the result of that disposition, not its cause. A great deal of stir was once made in New York by the assertion of a non-episcopal divine that the Baptismal Service of the Episcopal Church taught or implied the damnation of unbaptized infants. One should rather say that it implied the impossibility of the damnation of any infant. For it certifies God's gracious disposition to all mankind; he who redeemed all, calling each one into his Kingdom. Love is the root of Baptism, not wrath. And if God be for them, who can be against them? An earthly parent's neglect will certainly not abrogate a Heavenly Father's disposition, and we may leave all these morally immature souls securely in the arms of Him who declared, long years before a single child was baptized, "Of such is the Kingdom of Heaven."

Lest the very strong and repeated expressions in the Holy Scripture concerning the universal obligation of Baptism, and its necessity for entrance into the Kingdom of God, might seem to militate against this charitable view concerning unbaptized infants, involved in the Prayer Book service, it may here be well to remind ourselves that such Scriptural expressions apply to the Baptism of the conscious and converted subjects of it. Our own service for the Baptism of adults, after quoting our Lord's words to Nicodemus, proceeds with this exhortation: "Whereby ye may perceive the great necessity of this sacrament when it may be had." We are to recognize in this declaration of Christ to the ruler who came under the concealment of the darkness to confer with him, as well as in the exhortation of St. Peter to the converted on the day of Pentecost, and in other strong expressions of the New Testament, concerning the "answer of a good conscience towards God" in Baptism, allusion to the duty of the confession of Christ and enrolment under his leadership, as well as of belief in him and subjective trust to him. The birth "of water and of the spirit" corresponds to the affirmation of St. Paul, "With the heart man believeth unto righteousness, and with the mouth confession is made unto salvation." Thus the Scriptural expressions concerning Baptism involve the subjective as well as the objective element in it; i. e. the disposition of the recipient as well as the force of the act. For Baptism as generally treated in the New Testament relates to adult converts and is regarded as their admission into the Christian Church on the confession and acceptance of the faith of the Church. It is the divinely appointed mode of that confession. Therefore the Scriptural assertions concerning the receiving of Baptism involve the aspect of it as a confession, as the expression of a moral disposition and determination on the part of the baptized. The strong utterances of our Lord on the necessity of the open confession of his name, which run through all his teachings, enter as an element into his and his disciples' utterances on the necessity of Baptism. The members of the Kingdom must be born of the spirit inwardly, and of water, involving the confession of Christ, outwardly. They must be joined to the Master and to the Brotherhood. The indication of this confessional element of Baptism is found in the Baptismal Service for Infants in the Prayer Book in the answers of the sponsors, which promise for the child the fulfilment of that confession and the promise of obedience to God's holy will and commandments.

But the Baptism of infants in the Prayer Book speaks of it as a new birth before faith and confession are possible. Yes, that is its great privilege, and in order to gather its meaning we are to remember what birth is. It is not the beginning of life. Nothing is born which is not already living. Birth is that critical change in the history of a living being which ushers it into the sphere where alone its life can meet the conditions and influences essential to the full development of its latent powers. The Council of Ephesus, in giving the Blessed Virgin the much misunderstood, often mistranslated, and generally abused title of theotokos (θεοτόκος), meant to affirm the reality of the incarnation in the pre-natal as well as in the post-natal life of Jesus Christ. It was meant to assert that the Divine Word was incarnate before Jesus was born into his Kingdom, the world. And in analogy to this, Baptism, as new birth or regeneration, stands for the placing in its proper spiritual environment of the being already redeemed to God in Christ Jesus. It does not involve (as the declaration of the House of Bishops in 1871 pointed out) a change of moral character in souls as yet incapable of moral action, but it involves the engrafting of the already redeemed life into the body of Christ, his Church, to which the promise of his presence and of his guidance by his spirit is given; all which is fitted to educe normal moral character from the child's first conscious breath. Thus the ideal of the Christian Life according to the Baptismal Service of the Prayer Book is nurture, not conversion. When that ideal is not attained, conversion comes in of course, and of necessity. But the normal expectation is avoidance of its necessity, at least in that critical experience of it which reverses the whole trend and tone of the moral life, which has become immoral in its root. Children are not to be converted and become as men, but men are to be converted to become as little children.

Before, however, treating of that nurture, it may be well to remark that Baptism by introducing the redeemed soul into the family of God as its proper spiritual environment (constituting it a very member incorporate in the mystical body of God's Son, which is the blessed company of all faithful people) rejects that individualistic conception of Christian Life which makes religion merely personal, or exclusively individual. To assert that religion is simply a matter between God and the soul, is to the conception of the Common Prayer a partial truth. Religion is essentially a matter between God and the soul, but it is not only that. It involves relationship with other souls equally the recipients of God's grace; and it finds in that association and relationship, and in the ordinances which express it and bind it together, a most fruitful means of developing the individual Christian life. Baptism makes the normal Christian life to begin in a sense of companionship and relationship. As the infant comes to consciousness, it is, if he be rightly instructed as to his baptismal privilege, to the consciousness of membership in a sacred community, as being called unto and adopted into God's family of which Christ is the head. By the divine intention and provision and gracious gift, he is "a child of God, a member of Christ, and an inheritor of the Kingdom of Heaven." His part and duty is therefore response, the response of his own consent; and that response is fostered, stimulated, and in large part secured, through the mediating ministry of the church of which he finds himself a member, its instructions, its prayers, its sacraments made alive by the Holy Spirit and of God. His spiritual life is thus not wholly introspective, but is, so to speak, circumspective. It involves the sense of brotherhood and, as one of that brotherhood, of loyalty to Christ, just as inevitably as citizenship in the State involves the recognition of fellow citizens and the sharing of a common patriotism binding all to one country. Christian nurture, therefore, which infant Baptism involves, is not based solely on the idea of an isolated individual experience, but on the conception of participation in a family life.

CHAPTER XI

THE LESSON OF CONFIRMATION FOR THE CHRISTIAN LIFE

IN the order of the Church's discipine between the two sacraments, Baptism and the Lord's Supper, the Rite of Confirmation comes in. None of the Church's children, for whose nurture she is responsible, are to be admitted to the Holy Communion "until such time as they be confirmed or are ready and desirous to be confirmed," and the minister is "earnestly to move the Persons confirmed to come without delay to the Lord's Supper."

The light which Confirmation thus throws upon the Christian life is significant. It is, in itself, the official recognition and culmination of that Christian nurture which the sponsors in Baptism are pledged to secure to the baptized child. It emphasizes the subjective or confessional side of Baptism, while it is significant in the method of its administration of the great truth to which Baptism bears witness, that salvation comes not primarily of one's native resolution nor of the Christian knowledge and instruction one may have received, but of God's favor and goodness in the bestowal of the grace of his Holy Spirit. For Confirmation is "ministered," and that by the Chief Pastor of the flock, to "signify by the laying on of his hands, after the example of the holy Apostle, God's favor and gracious goodness towards them." But the essential preliminary of this Episcopal act is that " with their own mouth and consent openly before the church they ratify and confirm" what was promised for them in Baptism. That is, the baptized are both to confirm and to be confirmed. They are not to be confirmed until they confirm, until they, "having come to the years of discretion," have been thoroughly instructed in the Creed, the Lord's Prayer, and the Ten Commandments, and in the Catechism's exposition of the same, that they may be able intelligently to "ratify and confirm" the promises made for them in baptism, and "promise that by the grace of God they will evermore endeavor themselves faithfully to observe such things as they, by their own confession, have assented unto."

Confirmation therefore, as the act of the confirmed, bears witness that there must be subjective assent and response to the objective grace of God, witnessed to and sealed in Baptism, in order that that grace may prove effectual. And, as the church's act by the Bishop, it also bears witness that Confirmation is not only an assumption of responsibility on man's part, but that it is also an assurance of grace on God's part, who promises, as the laying on of the hands of the Bishop signifies, to "strengthen them with the Holy Ghost." Confirmation thus witnesses to both the duty and the privilege of the Christian life. It teaches that no effort of man to meet his responsibility but meets the responsive grace of God to enable him to accomplish it. While it marks the Christian life as sober, it makes it anything but sombre. It emphasizes its dignity as an intelligent service of God, which it characterizes as our bounden duty. It intensifies as well its exaltation and joy, in its recognition that God "worketh in us both to will and to do of his good pleasure," which constitutes its unspeakable privilege.

As so much in Confirmation and the Christian life depends upon Christian nurture, in order to understand the Prayer Book's conception of that life we must scrutinize the substance of the nurture unfolded in its pages. Now if we look not only at the responses and pledges of the sponsors in Baptism as indicating the demand and expectation of the Church in regard to the child which it receives, but also at the general tone of the services which it provides for its nutriment of worship, it becomes evident that emphasis is laid in the Common Prayer chiefly on "life as a blending of piety and morals"; piety, or the love of God, being the inspiring motive, and morality, or obedience to his will, being its indispensable manifestation. In the Catechism the Apostles' Creed (in its exhibition of God the Father, who made me, of God the Son, who redeemed me, of God the Holy Ghost, who sanctifieth me) is given as the inspiration of a life for God and in God. And God's holy will and commandments furnish the rule by which that inspiration is to guide the life. The stress is laid, not on emotion, but on the fulfilment of life's duties. The faith enjoined is not exhausted in *notitia*, perception of the truth, or *assensus*, acquiescence in the truth, but only in *fiducia*, trust to the truth. A "faith which works by love" is its command and demand.

In the Collects of the daily services the baptized is taught to pray that he may "so hear God's word," not only that he may understand it, but "that it may bring forth in him the fruit of good living"; that he may so receive God's guidance that "all his works may be begun, continued, and ended in him," that he may be so purified that he "may love the things which God commandeth"; that he may be so enlightened that he "may perceive and know what things he ought to do, and have grace and power faithfully to fulfil the same." "A life of love fulfilling the law," that is the undertone of the whole Book of Common Prayer. It is not a life of ecstasy, nor simply of orthodox acceptance of a creed, but a life of obedience, and its end is character; the Divine will interpenetrating and incorporating itself in the human will. One is to so "thankfully receive Christ's inestimable benefit of redemption as to daily endeavor himself to follow the blessed steps of his most holy life." That is the end and aim of the Christian nurture of the Prayer Book. As Dr. McConnell, in his stimulating History of the Episcopal Church, has well said: "Its purpose is to produce and conserve goodness. Its dominant tone is ethical rather than intellectual or emotional. It has often been taunted with 'lack of vital piety,' with worldliness, with cold morality. Dogmatists and emotionalists from within have attempted to transform her genius, but have not succeeded. The abiding instinct has kept her steadfast to her conception of the church as an Institute of Righteousness. This has determined her position towards doctrine, discipline, and worship, and fixed her conditions of membership and intercommunion. Her great test of the truth and value of doctrine is its immediate effect upon living. . . . Her liturgy is valued and insisted upon, not chiefly for its beauty or antiquity, or its fitness to express exalted emotions, but because of its disciplinary power to uphold the soul in right living. . . . The only condition on which she will turn the key of the Kingdom of Heaven to bind or loose is an ethical condition. She bids to the Holy Sacrament all those who 'do truly and earnestly repent them of their sins, and are in love and charity with their neighbors, and intend to lead a new life walking in the commandments of God.'"

While then the Christian life (according to the Prayer Book) is normally and primarily a life of righteousness, of character imbued with the spirit and mind of Christ, the services to which the baptized is introduced emancipate his conception of religion from the limitations of an isolated individualism, i. e. from regarding it simply as a personal concern. It comes to him in the form of a communal life. As a type of such service we need look only at the Litany, whose comprehensiveness of thought is unmatched save by the beauty of its diction. Its deprecations are very searching indeed regarding individual character and personal responsibility both temporal and eternal. Evil, mischief, sin, blindness of heart, pride, vainglory, hypocrisy, envy, hatred, malice, all uncharitableness, inordinate affections, deceits of world, flesh, and devil, hardness of heart, contempt of God's word and commandment, — from all these personal perversions of character, the reiterated response goes up, "Good Lord deliver us!" deliver us amid all life's joys and tribulations, in death's dark hour, and in the judgment day. But in the supplications we pass into a not less sacred, yet into a wider realm. The whole church emerges as the object of our care; the State with its rulers and magistrates, all the representatives of Christ's ministry, and all looking forward to that ministry, that they may be laborers and not drones; all people, all nations, a universal peace on sea and land, all the erring, all the deceived, the strong, the weak, the fallen, travellers on land and sea, the sick, the young, the imprisoned, orphans and widows, and the desolate and oppressed, and many more; all enter within the scope of supplication, and all thus become the objects of solicitous regard and aid. The horizon of religion is made coextensive with the horizon of life; and all life of the state and of society, as of the church, is regarded as a service of God. It is to be fashioned into a department of his kingdom, by infilling it with the Christian temper and the religious character. As soon then as one finds his true life he is led out beyond it, loses it, as it were, to find it multiplied and enlarged in other lives which it is to stimulate, and to which it is to minister. The whole tone of the Litany, as of the other offices of devotion in which the child is led in worship, is altruistic; altruistic not in that bald and excessive sense which stigmatizes the saving of one's own soul as selfish, and proclaims devotion to the souls of others the only true Christian devotion; but in the sense that the value of one's own soul (which according to the Master outweighs and outmeasures the whole terrestrial creation) is made the standard of the value of other souls, which are to be loved and treasured as one's own. To seek to save one's own soul is the least selfish of acts, if one catches the meaning of what its salvation is. That is surrender of the soul to God.

It is the saying, I will not live by myself, or for myself. I will live to him who loved me and gave himself for me. Such care is a first duty, and a transcendent duty. It is the only worthy return to God who gave the life to give it back to him to fashion and direct. But in its surrender to its Father is involved the surrender to the brotherhood as well. Living to him who loved me and gave himself for me, is to live also to these whom he loved, and for whom he gave and gives himself too. This is the true Gospel altruism, to love one's neighbor as one's self. There is a true self-consideration. It is one which does not end in self-consideration, but will consider all souls as members of one body.

The Christian life then which is regarded, as Baptism regards it, as a vocation of God, is one suffused with human sympathy and interpenetrated with mutual helpfulness. It will have none of that impassive cynicism which, declaring the laws of society inexorable, leaves those laws to work out their result unalleviated by human kindness, and declares that the result, exact and unerring though pitiless, is the only true benevolence, because the only benevolence of law. But religion recognizes a higher social law than the clashing and clanging of an impersonal social machinery. Personal character and destiny can never, according to the Christian faith, be wrought out by impersonal forces. Its moving power is not mechanic but dynamic. Spiritual influences alone are competent to evolve spiritual character. The building up of man, not as the supreme animal, but as a moral being whose self-determination constitutes him a spiritual character, must involve spiritual appeal to that self-determination. And that spiritual appeal is not only to the law of conscience, though it is that primarily, but is also the appeal of sympathy which is the law of life; the appeal of sympathy through helpfulness and sacrifice. There is a struggle for existence and a survival of the fittest in the moral as in the physical world, but that struggle is in its own atmosphere and on its own plane. The realm of this moral struggle is one where personal interest and heartfelt sympathy, and the helpfulness of the hands which manifest and impart them, are strong factors in the achievement. A political economy which leaves these out and regards them as mischievous intermeddling with a natural order which they disturb, but cannot destroy, is one which fails to recognize the spiritual side of life, which is its determining side. It is a Gradgrind theory which imprisons man within the bars of a terrestrial cage, instead of stimulating his flight in the atmosphere of spiritual realities. But life as a vocation of God, as Baptism declares it to be, is life in the realm of spiritual realities.

The spiritual altruism of the Christian nurture ministered in the Prayer Book has been a strong stimulus to the great humanitarian movement of modern times, which, though passing far beyond the ken of these ancient formularies, is yet a legitimate development of them. Their spirit of sympathy and helpfulness finds not a new home, but only a larger habitation, in these modern movements. These express in wiser and ampler form the old regard of the Litany for the imprisoned, the desolate, and the oppressed. Prison reform, tenement house reform, sanitation, societies for preventing cruelty to children and animals, homes for the rescue of the unfortunate, hospitals, reformatories, the thousand and one methods of bringing large relief to human misfortune in modern days, are simply enlarged and riper illustrations of the spirit which of old time offered in the Litany its petitions for the evils they mitigate.

Of course, there are great abuses possible on this helpful side of life. Alms may impoverish as well as help. Feeling is not always judicious, and there may be a false charity, which is like a spendthrift who is lavish in generosity, while he fails to pay his debts. But a mythical Micawber does not discredit a real Shaftesbury, and the Borrioboola Gha of the satirist does not lessen the power of the lives of Martyn and Hannington and Pattison in the actual course of the world. If the largess of others always pauperized, we must be all of us living in the poorhouse. For what have we that we have not received? The Fathers labored, and we are entered into their labors. No graduate of a college pays half the cost of his education. The benefactions of founders and endowers put him lastingly in their debt. The glories of architecture and literature and art are ours, as the free gift of former generations. Generosity may sometimes relax the muscles of exertion, but indifferent avarice chills the life blood. Humanity can never rise to its ideal and normal life save as it recognizes life's divine vocation, and its consequent ministries of sympathy and helpfulness; and this is the teaching of the Book of Common Prayer.

CHAPTER XII

THE LORD'S SUPPER IN ITS BEARING ON THE CHRISTIAN LIFE

A LIFE so noble in its inspiration, and so wide in its scope of gracious ministration, as we have seen Baptism and its correlated nurture imply, must surely require a vast increment of strength. Amid a world of temptation and with the inherent trend to self-indulgence, where self-gratification is easy and duty often looms before us as the

> "Stern daughter of the voice of God,"

is there nothing in the church which stands for divine strength, as well as for a divine vocation?

We turn to consider this element of the normal Christian life as taught and embodied in the sacrament of the Lord's Supper. For this great sacrament stands, to every point of view from which men look at it, for the divine nutriment of the Christian life. Its very outward gesture and deed presuppose the impossibility of retaining and developing spiritual strength without heavenly food, as really as the impossibility of maintaining natural life without physical food. And that heavenly food it sets forth as no less than the very life of the redeeming Master imparted unto us. This sacrament is the strongest possible witness to the high and divine nature of man's spiritual life, in that it declares both that man is capable of sharing that life and that his life is abnormal and stunted and unnatural (by the standard of his true nature) if he do not share it. It indicates the reasonableness, while it does not detract from the grace, of that great redemption by the cross which it celebrates, in that, while it sets forth its imperative necessity, it reveals how splendidly worth saving that manhood is which is thus capable of receiving so divine a guest, and which lives its only true life in his blest companionship. For without entering into the sphere of controversy concerning the method and measure of this sacrament, the simple contemplation of its essential features shows the vivid relation in which it brings man's spiritual life to the life whose sacrifice of itself it celebrates. On its divine side this service is rooted in the great objective fact of Christ's sacrificial death for man; on man's side, in that devout remembrance of it which is a participation in it: "Do this in remembrance of me. Take, eat, drink ye all of this." Thus the Master, and so the Apostle: "As often as ye eat this bread and drink this cup ye do show the Lord's death till he come. The cup of blessing which we bless, is it not the communion of the blood of Christ? The bread which we break, is it not the communion of the body of Christ?"

By rejecting the doctrine of Transubstantiation, our church has removed the words of consecration from the realm of the literal and physical to that of the spiritual and vital. In affirming that transubstantiation is not only an imperfect but a false doctrine, one not simply obscuring, but overthrowing the nature of a sacrament, it has followed our Lord's own commentary on his words concerning eating his flesh and drinking his blood. Great and essential as is the truth conveyed by those asserting words, our Lord declared they were to be taken spiritually, not physically.

To his wondering and perplexed disciples, startled by his strong declaration, "Except ye eat the flesh of the Son of Man and drink his blood, ye have no life in you," he answered, "Doth this offend you? . . . It is the Spirit that quickeneth; the flesh profiteth nothing: the words that I speak unto you, they are spirit and they are life." This exposition of his words by the Master himself gives the sense in which the Communion Service of the Prayer Book receives and utters them. The Ritual uses freely the Lord's language, but always in consonance with his spiritual explanation of it. According to this the words of Consecration embody and declare the great spiritual truth, the basis of all true Christian life, that Christ's followers must live in him by his living in them. They lift the sacrament and the soul which celebrates it into the atmosphere and power of the Lord's presence. They do not indeed imply or promise a physical manifestation or impartation of him. His presence in the flesh he had himself declared it was expedient should be removed, that his presence by the Spirit might be the more real and effectual in his followers. But the word and action of the Sacrament both indicate and guarantee that inward spiritual participation in his life and nature which is the essential source of spiritual life. "I in them and they in me," the service is ever saying as we receive the consecrated bread and wine, the sacred symbols of his body and his blood: the outward and visible sign lifting us into the region of the invisible and eternal reality.

The sacrament on man's part is "the memorial which Christ hath commanded us to make." This remembrance of him in his death and passion is the subjective condition of receiving within us that life which he alone possesses and can alone impart. That life, the life which he laid down for us, he vouchsafes to give to hearts made ready to receive him by obeying his command, "Do this in remembrance of me." To them he fulfils the gracious promise, "He that cometh to me shall never hunger, and he that believeth on me shall never thirst." To this act of obedient and grateful love he responds by the fulfilment of the wondrous word, uttered in the hour of the institution of this sacrament, "If any man love me he will keep my word, and my Father will love him, and we will come and make our abode with him."

This rooted remembrance, which is the element which man contributes to a real communion, is one of the deepest mysteries, while it is one of the most assured realities of man's spiritual nature. The fact of memory is one which attests the continuity of man's being, and shatters the senseless theory that he is a mere succession of sensations with no enduring personality in which they inhere. The power of the recall of the past so as to make it the influence of the present, is the indubitable testimony to the reality and the real continuity of that past and present. Memory, thus testifying to personality, becomes the purveyor of spiritual forces and influences. It is the personality enriching its present life with the treasures stored up by its past experiences, making of these past experiences not dead relics of a vanished life, but principalities and powers of the life that now is and is to come. To this great spiritual faculty of man, Christ appeals when he would make his life and sacrifice living realities of man's spiritual experience.

This remembrance in the Sacrament of the body and blood of Christ is, as set forth in the communion service, threefold. It is first of all individual, a remembrance in the mind of the believer. He calls to remembrance what Christ is to him through the gift of that life and death for him. He communes with him in his heart, and his presence is very real. But not only individually and in the secret recesses of his being is this remembrance held. It is a remembrance in and with the community of the faithful; a common remembrance, therefore a remembrance which is a celebration, or common participation in the remembrance; the commemoration of the church which is the blessed company of all faithful people. "We do celebrate," as the phrase in the Oblation asserts. As in the lower yet still sacred circle of the family not only the individual child remembers and hallows the mother's birthday, but all the children together celebrate it, and thus add to the power of the personal remembrance by the common family participation; as in the divinely ordered state the patriot not only recalls the national anniversary, but celebrates it with his fellow citizens, enhancing and deepening his individual allegiance by participation in the common patriotism; so in this far more sacred family, in this high and holy nation, the great underlying fact of its redemption comes in power through a common remembrance of it, of which this holy sacrament is a celebration. And then the third element of the remembrance enters. We not only remember in our hearts, and remember with others in the common celebration, but we remember before God; "we celebrate and make here before thy Divine Majesty the memorial thy Son hath commanded us to make." So the word proceeds. The earthly service begun in the silent chamber of the heart ends by ushering us into the court of heaven. And we make the memorial there, not indeed to remind the Father of that eternal fact, deep down in his own eternal being, of the "Lamb slain from the foundation of the world," which is as eternally present to his mind as it is eternally present in his heart, but to declare our remembrance of it as the ground of our approach and as the plea for our participation in the grace here set forth. With the divinely ordered sacramental symbols of that dying love, we represent before the Father that all-sufficient sacrifice whose merit we now plead in act, as we plead it in word, in every prayer we utter for Christ's sake, our hearts attuned to the strain so nobly rendered by Canon Bright in his communion hymn:

> "And now, O Father, mindful of the love
> Which bought us, once for all, on Calvary's tree,
> And having with us him who pleads above,
> We here present, we here set forth to thee
> That only offering perfect in thine eyes,
> That one true, pure, immortal sacrifice."

And thus the memorial of that one great and sufficient sacrifice becomes on our part a spiritual sacrifice, a sacrifice of praise and thanksgiving for its love and benefit, of intercession for its grace and merit, and of surrender in its spirit and through its power of ourselves, "our souls and bodies, to be a reasonable, holy, and living sacrifice" unto him, which is, though we are unworthy to offer any sacrifice, our bounden duty and service.

I have striven briefly to condense the essential elements of the service of the Holy Communion into such statement as seems to me to be the clear indication and meaning of our ritual, in order to indicate more clearly the normal Christian life to which it bears witness. The whole service is one common to priest and people, not something done by one for the other, but all remembering, all celebrating, all communicating, and all offering the spiritual sacrifices of love and praise and prayer and consecration, though one be officially set as the priestly mouthpiece of the priestly people. The appeal of this sacrament is to the life of every one, and its assertion is positive of a life of God in man to-day, through the faith which is in Christ Jesus, who loved us and gave himself for us. For nothing testifies to the object and the nature of the Christian's faith by which he lives more than this service, which speaks of Christ's real presence as the very food of the soul. The faith which is the root of the normal Christian life is not primarily a faith in statement, but in fact. It does not rest ultimately in dogma, or description, but in him whom the dogma portrays in some element of his being or function of his office. It is not the believing about him, but the trusting in him. The dogma, like the law, may be the schoolmaster, but its office and use are to lead to Christ.

Neither does faith, as set forth in the Eucharist, rest in the Church, the body of Christ, for it looks beyond the body to the spirit of the Lord, which, if it do not share, it is (as the Apostle says) none of his. As his body and his bride the Church is very sacred, and, as we have seen, ministers, as it was intended to minister if rightly used, very potentially to the life of the spirit. But it is not the *terminus ad quem* of the Christian life. If true to itself, it points beyond itself. Behold, it cries not me, but "Behold the Lamb of God, who taketh away the sin of the world." Both dogma, the mind of the church, and ritual, its discipline, are to the one great end, " Christ formed within you." They are like the telescope and spectroscope in relation to the heavenly bodies. They are not primarily to be looked at, (though their correct construction and accurate preservation are most important factors in their use,) but they are chiefly to be looked through. It is the heavenly vision they disclose to which we are to be obedient. The great value and function of the Church is not to monopolize attention, but to bring the soul face to face with Him whose Church it is.

The faith thus portrayed as essential by the sacrament of the Lord's Supper is a living faith in a living Lord. The life to which it points is a life which "stands fast in the liberty wherewith Christ hath made us free," a life which because of that liberty finds a necessity laid upon it, the necessity of grateful love, to consecrate itself Christ's faithful soldier and servant unto its life's end.

Is not this, it may be asked, an ideal of life overwrought, overstrained, of necessity remote from life's rough tasks and common companionships; a life unlike that which is indicated in Baptism as a divine vocation to contend with the sins and cruelties, neglects and injustices, of the world; the life of encounter, for guidance and safe conduct in which we pray in the Litany and all the Prayer Book services? But the answer is, "a life remote only in its source." And the very source from which the life springs points not to seclusion and quiet ecstasy, but to vigorous and manly endeavor, to a life masterful in its conquests as virile in its undertakings. "By thy Baptism, Fasting, and Temptation. By thine Agony and Bloody Sweat." The divine strength manifest in these stern experiences is the strength sought and found in Christ, and sought and found for like conflict and like victory.

And thus through its sacraments, as through all its offices, the Prayer Book indicates the nature of the normal Christian life. It is a life of Divine vocation, of Divine companionship, of manly development in virtue and knowledge, of expanding strength and widening vision, of rational confidence, of bold encounter, of expectant victory; a life in Christ and with Christ and for Christ, "till we all come in the unity of the faith, and of the knowledge of the Son of God, unto a perfect man, unto the measure of the stature of the fulness of Christ, . . . of whom the whole family in heaven and earth is named."

CHAPTER XIII

CLERGY AND LAITY — THE MINISTRY OF INSTRUCTION

THE Christian Life as conceived in the Prayer Book is not only one of Christian association, involved in the general conception of it as membership in Christ's Church. The Church is an organized society, and while every member of the same has his vocation and ministry of mutual helpfulness, there are those especially set apart for the service of the brotherhood in things pertaining to the religious life. In fine, there is an official distinction of the clergy and laity involving a distinctive relation of the two. The peculiar people are by reason of their vocation a royal priesthood, but there is also an official priesthood representative of them, consecrated to act in behalf of the priestly people towards God, and to act for God in special forms of ministration for the people. The mutual life of all Christians must be orderly. Let all things be done decently and in order is the Apostle's command, and "order is the parent of orders." It is well known (and as this is not an ecclesiastical treatise it need only be mentioned without being defended or enlarged upon) that the Prayer Book in its Ordinal and in all its offices assumes the existence of the threefold ministry of bishops, priests, and deacons as valid from the times of the Apostles. It emphasizes the importance of the preservation of this order in its historic integrity, so that "no man shall be suffered in this Church to execute any of said functions unless he . . . has had Episcopal consecration or ordination."

What we are to consider is the bearing of this ministry upon the Christian life, and to mark the conception of that life as evinced by this discipline to which it is subjected in order to its successful development.

The conception of the Christian Life of the Clergy is set forth in the Ordinal, which contains the offices of their consecration; that of the Christian people as related to the clergy is indicated in the rubrical directions, which regulate the common worship of both.

As we study the Ordinal and the Rubrics, the oneness of the religious life common to all estates of men in Christ's Church comes at once into prominence. The same faith, the same diligence, the same consecration of the life to the Master, the same following of the Saviour's steps, are enjoined equally upon all men. The sanctity of one is the sanctity of all. The difference of office does not affect in the least the essence of the Christian Life, it only touches the outer form of some of its activities. The clergy as portrayed in the Prayer Book are not a caste, exempt from the demands to which the laity must succumb, or deprived of rights which the laity may claim. In all the essential features of religious living clergy and laity are called to the same task and endowed with the same privileges. If we connote the exhortations of the Baptismal and Ordination services we find the same ideal of religious character held up to all alike, "which is, to follow the example of our Saviour Christ, and to be made like unto him; continually mortifying all our evil and corrupt affections, and daily proceeding in all virtue and godliness of living." This, which is from the Baptismal office, is in complete unison with the ordination promise to "deny all ungodliness and worldly lusts, and live soberly, righteously, and godly in this present world," and indicates that unity of spirit amid differences of ministration which finds utterance in the prayer contained in the office of the "Ordering of Priests," in these words: "that as well by these thy ministers, as by them over whom they shall be appointed thy ministers, thy Holy Name may be forever glorified and thy blessed Kingdom enlarged."

The vocation of the clergy then, as that of the laity, is to what may be called a natural spiritual life. They are to be of the people in their mode of religious living; for the natural relations of life are of divine institution, and are not barriers to the Master's approach, but means through which he enters into communion with the soul. Thus, in the questions of the ordination examination it is taken for granted that the clergy share and mingle in the common life. "Will you be diligent to frame and fashion your own selves and *your families*, according to the Doctrine of Christ?" it is asked. Celibacy, or exclusion from ordinary family ties, is not of the essence of the clerical character. There may be times when it is proper and expedient for a clergyman to remain single, as is also true for the laity. Such exigency is not exclusively clerical.

St. Paul evidently considered the exigencies of his time as giving great weight to the value of the single life. But the references to this subject by the Apostle, and by his Master and ours, are to a temporary expedient. There is no superior sanctity in celibacy, so that the clergy who are to be ensamples to the flock must practise it. The clergy and the laity are co-workers together for one and the same object, and are not to be separate in their sympathies or to be kept apart through diverse disciplines.

What light then does the existence of clergy and laity throw upon the nature of the religious life which they share in common? It shows, first of all, the serious nature of that life in its deep need of guidance and discipline and instruction for its adequate development. Christian life is not a holiday pastime. Man in religion is called to a high and strenuous endeavor. That life is likened pre-eminently in Scripture to a warfare, in relation to evil within and without, to a race, in reference to its arduous and necessary attainment, to a taking of the yoke, which symbolizes obedient service. A ministry divinely set to accomplish a discipline of instruction and worship is a perpetual witness to the sober task of religion; it inbreathes the earnest mind, and divests its atmosphere of all trace of ease, or carelessness, or indifference. It marks the religious life as supreme both in the dignity of its aim and in the strenuousness of its effort. The ministry which is appointed for the service of the body of believers emphasizes the necessity of that service, and ennobles it as worthy the enterprise of earnest minded men. Yet it does not in witnessing to religion as sober make it sombre. Its voice is a voice of cheer as well as of exhortation. Its presence testifies to its task, but to its hopefulness as well. It is a witness to need, but also to relief. While it depicts the Christian life as one involving earnest and unremitting effort, it discloses as well the reality of a divine interest and aid to make that effort effectual. Why is the ministry placed in the midst of Christ's Church? "I am among you," said Christ of himself, "as one that serveth." His presence was itself a confession of human need, but it was a revelation as well of divine rescue. Such also is the testimony of his ministry. The clergy are for necessary service, but are appointed for hopeful service. Christ has set them in the church. They are not the mere evidence of a human want which created them, and threw them up on the surface of its necessity. They are the sign of the divine interest which appointed them. "He gave some apostles, some prophets, some evangelists, and some pastors and teachers for the perfecting of the Saints, for the work of the ministry, for the edifying of the body of Christ." So the very presence of the ministry testifies to Christ's presence and care, and the Christian life thus guarded may well be a life of aspiration, of enthusiasm, of joyful anticipation, because a life which God has set himself so sedulously to protect and develop. It makes life sacred to find it so carefully tended, and brings the sense of a divine companionship into it, as one which Christ watches. Its immeasurable worth is disclosed in the fact that God so ardently desires to bring it to perfection.

This is the more impressed on us when we come to note not only that the ministry is, but what it is. How is it to aid the Divine life in man? What light do its functions shed on the Christian Life it fosters?

First take its element of instruction. The ministry are especially appointed to be preachers by the authority which established them. "Preach my Gospel to every creature" accompanies the Apostles' commission to go into all the world, and forms the first element of it. St. Paul avers that "it pleased God by the foolishness of preaching to save them that believe." What preaching means we gather from the letters of the first great preachers, which we call Epistles, and which let us into the very life of the early Church. Preaching according to these ensamples is not merely the recitation of gospel facts, but the application of them in their principles to the daily life and changing circumstances of men. The pulpit stands for applied Christianity. Its object is not merely the statement of a mystery, but a flooding of life with the light of the mystery. It is not so much an explaining of life as suffusing it with a sense of heavenly worth and glory by reason of the mystery of godliness revealed to it in the Gospel preached. It is showing how the least things of life may be done in the spirit of the greatest, through the inspiration from on high. Preaching, in fine, is bringing Christ to bear on daily life. Amid all the divineness of its heavenly vision, it is meant to keep life steadfast and efficient as a work among men and a work for men. And yet by its unfolding of the sublime truths of the Gospel it wards off all taint of dreariness and lifeless routine from duty, because of its stimulus to an intelligent apprehension of the faith.

Preaching thus is meant to keep faith practical and to elevate practice into a living energy of love. Its legitimate tendency is to discriminate religion from superstition through the intelligence with which it illumines it, and to make life religious through the divine vision and mandate with which it confronts it. It is an amazing witness by its very function to life as a walk with God, for it constantly proclaims his law and presents his truth afresh in its bearing on the duty of the hour. It may become very dead and prosy by declining into a mere repetitious statement of worn out arguments and abstract dogmas. But it is meant to be daily bread for daily living; not a discipline of the schools, but a converse with those by the wayside of life. It is fitted to impart that ideal impulse to actual life which comes only of the association of its common tasks, its petty cares, its vexing perplexities, its blinding sorrows, its successes and its joys, with a life above and beyond itself, "a life hid with Christ in God." Hence the value of a ministry whose members are partakers of the common life, as well as scholars in the truths of God.

CHAPTER XIV

THE MINISTRY OF CONSOLATION

WHILE preaching is a great function of the ministry, it is not its only function. There is the ministry of official as well as of personal declaration, wherein the clergyman speaks, by reason of his office, the authoritative message of God to his people. This lies in the ministration of the sacraments and the declaration of absolution. As elsewhere we have treated of the Christian Life as illustrated in the sacraments, let us here look at the declaration of absolution, as taught in the Prayer Book, in its elucidation of the Christian Life.

In what does one find the root principle of the Christian Life? Is it not in the fact of forgiveness, or of God's coming to the soul in reconciliation? If all God's revelation of himself in Christ were simply to show a divine excellence in human nature, it might awaken a boundless admiration in human souls, but it would prove anything rather than a ministry of consolation to human life. For the fact of sin is a root fact in human consciousness and experience. There lies in each soul, as it comes to know itself, the sense of defect of goodness, and the perception of that law in the members which wars against the law of the mind, bringing us into captivity to the law of sin. The supreme want of human life is to reach God as a sinner. We must come to him in reconciliation. There must be in the Divine Mind the element of forgiveness if there is human help there. The Christ who comes to impart life must come to the world to save sinners, else he does not reach us. The fundamental fact from which all growth into godliness proceeds is the fact that in Christ God is reconciling the world unto himself; and that to each soul he is saying, "Thy sins are forgiven thee." His advent, to awaken in men immortal hope, must be the tacit declaration: "No taint of hereditary tendency to evil, repugnant to me as that trend of nature is; no actual yielding to the law of sin, setting the human will against my own, hateful as this wilful trangression is; no mystery of iniquity in man, in fine, shall suffice to quench the mystery of godliness in Christ, who taketh away the sin of the world." He comes in order to reveal the eternal heart of God in which the Christ is as a "Lamb slain from the foundation of the world." Believing in God, as seen in Christ, as one who in the face of all sin, original and actual, seeks to join man's soul to himself, who bids men love him because he first loved them, the soul gains power to lead a new life. The longing for that new life rises, the strength to gain it rises, the ideal of it rises. A sinful life may become a life hid with Christ in God. All the future Christian life is thus contained in the seed of forgiveness.

In the ministry of reconciliation the declaration of the fact of Divine forgiveness must be made a fundamental feature. And the record of the Gospel meets this necessity. Christ after his resurrection gave command that "repentance and remission of sins should be preached in his name among all nations," and he declared to his disciples, as he breathed on them, "whosesoever sins ye remit they are remitted unto them, and whosesoever sins ye retain they are retained." However we construe these words, they set the fact and doctrine of forgiveness in the very forefront of Christian truth.

The Prayer Book meets this fundamental want in its Declaration of Absolution contained in the daily offices of morning and evening prayer, and in the weekly office of the administration of the Holy Communion. Its interpretation of the words of the Risen Lord to his disciples, "Whosesoever sins ye remit they are remitted unto them, and whosesoever sins ye retain they are retained," is found in its provision for carrying them into effect. Both the rubric which directs the manner of its use and the words themselves of the Declaration of Absolution show the mind of the Anglican Communion in regard to the function of the ministry in relation to the forgiveness of sins. The Declaration follows the confession of sin and the prayer for forgiveness. Then the priest rises to give the assurance of God's attitude and disposition towards the repentant sinner, and of Christ's commission to his ministers authoritatively to declare that disposition. The fact of forgiveness is not to remain doubtful to any penitent soul. "He pardoneth and absolveth all those who truly repent and unfeignedly believe his Holy Gospel"; the Gospel of forgiveness. God's attitude and act are sure. He for his part will most surely keep and perform them. And in view of this Divine certainty the sinful soul is bidden to ask for the grace of true penitence by the Holy Spirit, that its repentance may give free course to the mercy of God, that it may be glorified in man's deliverance according to the will of God. To make this positive and authoritative declaration is inherent in the ministerial commission, and the fact that it is so is a strong attestation to the individual soul of the general fact of forgiveness contained in the Gospel. Whosoever thus accepts the fact thus declared, his sins are remitted, whosoever refuses, his sins are retained; but sins are remitted by the mercy of God only through man's own act of acceptance, and they are retained in spite of

God's mercy only by man's own act of refusal. The ministerial function in the act of forgiveness, is thus not the conveyance of forgiveness but the authoritative attestation that God forgives. The priest stands in his office as the commissioned witness to that attitude and disposition of God which welcomes penitent sinners.

The fundamental want then of man in coming to God in reconciliation is thus ministered to by the declaration of absolution in a most effective way. The essential element of the Gospel of Christ, forgiveness, is taken up into the worship of the Church and made prominent and personal to men then and there. The fact would be true, forever true, by Christ's word in the Gospel, were it not made conspicuous in the worship of the church. It is not true because the minister declares it, but the minister declares it because it is true, and he has power and commandment to declare it because it is a truth so essential to the Christian Life of every soul. The precatory form of the declaration of absolution in the communion service is based on the fundamental position elucidated in the declaration in the morning and evening prayer. Its wording is not so strong as the longer form, but it is essentially the same in meaning.

The whole tone and act of the service of the Prayer Book in this regard are most healthful. The confession is not to or through the priest, but with the priest to God, and the declaration by the priest is for himself as well as for the people. He as priest announces officially to himself as sinful man the same great truth of God on the same condition. His function is not the conveyance of the fact, but the conveyance of the knowledge and assurance of the fact, with and by the authority of the Great Master, who sealed the fact of forgiveness in his own blood. Thus the Christian Ministry stands in its very office for the great fact, that God in Christ is reconciling the world unto himself. And in this as in his other ministrations the minister's function is to bring men directly face to face with God, "unto whom all hearts are open, all desires known." Confession is directly to God, pardon is direct from him. The priest stands as the authoritative witness to this direct relation of God to man in the authoritative declaration which he makes of it. Auricular confession, which makes confession of sin through the priest essential, is a discipline which came into no part of the Church until after many centuries. It found its first Synodical authorization at the Fourth Lateran Council, A. D. 1215. The primitive Church did not practise it. The Prayer Book makes no general provision for it. In some extreme and exceptional condition, where by self-examination the individual cannot quiet his own conscience, he is told, in one of the occasional exhortations in the communion service, to go to some minister of God's word and open his grief that he may receive "such godly counsel and advice as may tend to the quieting of his conscience." But this is not in order to render God's pardon more efficacious because spoken by his minister, but to render repentance more efficacious by the minister's instruction of the sinner. It is a discipline for man's approach to God, not a medium of God's approach to man.

The Prayer Book of the English Church

speaks of the benefit of absolution as well as ghostly counsel and advice, and there is given for such cases a form of personal absolution, to be found in the private Office for the Visitation of the Sick. Both the phrase and the form were omitted from the American Prayer Book, doubtless for fear of fostering the notion that only through sacerdotal mediation could pardon be obtained for such extreme cases. That could not indeed have been the meaning of the English Book, which in its daily service so exclusively employs the declarative rather than the communicative form of absolution, and whose whole spirit is to affirm that the intervention of the priest is not needed between the soul and God. Its key note, as that of our own Prayer Book, is, "I will arise and go to my Father, and will say unto Him, Father, I have sinned." Its declaration of absolution, as ours, is, "He pardoneth and absolveth all those who truly repent and unfeignedly believe." Its general regimen is public confession, and, if there be an exception in some extreme case allowed, it is not allowed in order to overthrow and repudiate the doctrine and attitude affirmed and maintained in its daily offices of devotion, but simply to "minister to a mind diseased" that it too may escape from its morbidness and come to grasp the significance of the declaration of absolution, before all the people, that God himself effectively pardons the soul which comes directly in penitence to him. The priesthood are witnesses not mediators, declarers not conveyers of his grace. This runs all through the services of whatever nature which the Prayer Book furnishes in its delineation of the relation of priest and people.

The whole tone and expression of the Collects illustrate this attitude. The Collect for Ash Wednesday, to be repeated each day in Lent, is a very patent instance as intended for the specially penitent season of the Christian Year, and it stands in complete harmony with all the other Collects of the Book: "Almighty and Everlasting God, who hatest nothing that thou hast made, and dost forgive the sins of all those who are penitent, create and make in us new and contrite hearts that we worthily lamenting our sins and acknowledging our wretchedness may obtain of thee, the God of all mercy, perfect remission and forgiveness, through Jesus Christ our Lord." A Book which abounds in such prayers, which makes no provision for the instruction of private confessors, and contains no hint of the secret discipline of the confessional, which bids its ministers authoritatively to declare publicly each day to all people, that God "pardoneth and absolveth all who truly repent and unfeignedly believe," may truly claim to put the doctrine of forgiveness openly in the forefront of its delineation of the Christian Life. It moreover associates that doctrine with the co-ordinate truth that the Christian Life is an immediate relation of the soul to God, which requires no priestly mediation to make it effective. The one only Mediator according to it is He who, being both God and man, has broken down every barrier suggestive of indirect and difficult approach to the Father reconciled in Him.

The tone of the Prayer Book moreover in every part in regard to sin, while solemn, is that of solemn hopefulness. It is hopeful, for it is the witness of reconciliation. Its De

Profundis and its Magnificat run into each other. It speaks of cheer, though it speaks to sinners. How radiant is the Service of Holy Communion especially with hope and blessing! It is interpenetrated with the assurance that where sin abounded grace doth much more abound; that "not as the offence so also is the free gift; for if through the offence of one many be dead, much more the grace of God and the gift by grace, which is by one man, Jesus Christ, hath abounded unto many." It is full of comfortable words to the sinful, for they are words to the redeemed. It seems to be singing as its Eucharistic hymn: "Beloved, now are we the Sons of God, and it doth not yet appear what we shall be, but we know that when He doth appear we shall be like Him, for we shall see Him as he is." The Christian Life which it presupposes and to which it ministers has so deep a root in the loving and forgiving heart of God, that it is fully furnished with motive, stimulus, and inspiration to fight the good fight of faith and lay hold on eternal life.

www.ingramcontent.com/pod-product-compliance
Lightning Source LLC
Chambersburg PA
CBHW032152160426
43197CB00008B/878